The Truth about Trauma and Dissociation

To David
for his solidity, insight and kindness

Valerie Sinason

The Truth about Trauma and Dissociation

Everything
You Didn't Want to Know
and Were Afraid to Ask

CONFER
BOOKS

First published in 2020 by Confer Books, London

www.confer.uk.com

Registered office:
21 California, Martlesham, Woodbridge, Suffolk IP12 4DE, England

1 3 5 7 9 10 8 6 4 2

This is a work of nonfiction. Any similarity between the characters and situations
within its pages, and places, persons, or animals living or dead, could be
unintentional and co-incidental. Some names and identifying details have been
changed or omitted to, in part, protect the privacy of individuals.

British Library Cataloguing in Publication Data. A catalogue record for this book is
available from the British Library.

ISBN: 978-1-913494-08-7 (paperback)
ISBN: 978-1-913494-09-4 (ebook)

Typeset by Bespoke Publishing Ltd
Printed in the UK by Ashford Colour Press

CONTENTS

CONTENTS

ACKNOWLEDGEMENTS

With thanks to Marsha for reading and editing, to Sandy Dilip for her invaluable aid, to Brett Kahr for suggesting this, to the wonderful team at Confer Books , Christina Wipf Perry, Liz Wilson and Julie Bennett, for giving me a voice and making it as clear as it could be, to Jamie Keenan of Keenan Design and to all the brave people whose understanding speaks through me.

PREFACE

And when we speak we are afraid
Our words will not be heard
Nor welcomed
But when we are silent
We are still afraid
So it is better to speak
Remembering
We were never meant to survive

Audre Lorde, *The Black Unicorn: Poems*, 1995

Everyman,
I will go with thee,
and be thy guide,
In thy most need
to go by thy side.

From an anonymous medieval play, said by Knowledge
and used for each Everyman book from Dent publishers.

It can be hard to speak in difficult times, as well as hard to
hear. The voice of trauma, even when whispered, can hurt
the speaker and the listener. We need to be accompanied

at difficult and dangerous times in our lives. We need this, whether our attachment figures are human, spiritual, bird or other animals. Or, in our current time, as a brave and traumatised adult told me, there are also non-animate companions and guides. 'There is my iPhone. It is my brain, my heart, my memory and my guardian angel. It puts on a torch light when it is dark. It lets me call safe people. It provides music and pictures; tells me the time and it is always there. Not like therapy. Not like social services. Not like refuges. It doesn't close at Christmas.' Or the child, clutching his worn teddy bear, 'Teddy went into the bad places with me and the bad man hurt him worse.' We all need company in these complex days and especially when thinking about trauma.

This book is a guided tour of pain, of trauma that comes into us from the outside and its internal and external consequences that can continue for generations. It is a guide given by a wounded healer, who has been educated by the professors of pain, those with lived experience, as we all are also to whatever degree. We know it. We recognise the landscape. We have heard it and felt it and yet we do not wish to know what we know. Reality is too painful. As Philips stated (1995, p.34), 'the analyst has to enable the patient to know what he already knows'; and the patient/client has to drip-feed trauma to check out the capacity of the analyst or therapist until the words and thinking break through the relational mind.

Follow the path of this book with me as I try, within the limits of my own capacity, to stay mentally present with the contradictory enormity and simplicity of this subject.

The same points that we know and don't want to know appear and reappear in different ways and different layers to try to bypass our dissociative defences.

Dip in and out. Look after yourselves.

Thank you for being willing to try to hear.

There are rewards for this journey. We appreciate the world in a real, non-delusional way, and we appreciate the kindness of others even more.

The coronavirus and other plagues

Lord! How sad a sight it is to see the streets so empty of people.

Samuel Pepys, 16 August 1665

I did endeavour all I could to talk with as few as I could, there being now no observation of shutting up of houses infected, that to be sure we do converse and meet with people that have the plague.

Samuel Pepys, 14 September 1665

I am fain to allow myself [alcohol] during this plague time ... my physician being dead.

Samuel Pepys, 15 September 1665

As this book was being written, the conditions in which I wrote were of shielding. I and my husband are over 70 and therefore more vulnerable to our 2020 plague – coronavirus.

Most of us, whatever our age and background, are facing,

with a twenty-first-century plague, something that we never expected. For those of us lucky enough to not live through a war, this is a close second, even though the enemy is invisible and we do not see bloodshed in the streets or hear the explosion of bombs. Instead, the nightly mortality lottery, in which the numbers of the newly dead are reported, can be viewed dissociatively in the comfort of one's own home. What do the numbers of dead mean to us? Faces of loss and anguish flit before us, sandwiched by scientific and political discourse.

The British Prime Minister has been using the language of war, and so is the National Health Service (NHS) because the coronavirus kills wherever it can. It needs no passport and initially appeared to recognise no national, religious, gender, age or class boundaries. It has great productivity and works hard day and night to protect itself and expand its territory. Indeed, if it was not so lethal to us, we could admire it! However, although all of us risk death, the consequences are not equal, and nor are the chances of being infected. We hear of age and underlying conditions increasing vulnerability but very few mentions of mental health conditions, loneliness, poverty, terror of bankruptcy, stigma, living with abusers, bringing up children with no resources ... Poor areas have a greater risk, and so do people from BAME (Black, Asian and minority ethnic) backgrounds. In a strange way, the earliest and most effective containment for the

2

country was provided by those over the age of 90 – the Queen, David Attenborough, Vera Lynn and Captain Tom. Great-grandparents were needed, let alone grandparents.

Faced with something so unprecedented, there was a longing for wise, elderly people who had lived through a war, were self-contained and stoical, and told the truth. Perhaps the death wish to the over-70s ('Oh, it is only people over 70 dying a little earlier than usual') is atoned for by being grateful for those who have survived death wishes and death! Perhaps too, in an age of disinformation and fear of trans-parency, the retired and old people were the only voices to trust in this time of change.

Whatever our family circumstances, whatever our situa-tion, the medical appointment, the meeting, the get-together, the social event of the year, the wedding, the party, the sports event, the conference, the walk together, travel and holidays, holding the new baby, all these issues through which our identities have been formed, reconfirmed and enriched, have been on hold. Even touch, the most basic need for intimacy, has been compromised. All intimacy becomes cyber-intimacy. Orbach's seminal work on bodies (2002) takes on further meaning. She wondered if we would be the last generation to have bodies that were familiar to us. She looked at how, although the body is observed with more intensity than ever before, it is also dematerialised. Coronavirus has added to

3

this. The body is weak and can die but it is so powerful it can kill others, just by coughing. Will knife crime go down now that a cough can become a lethal weapon?

How have we dealt with this? If we are lucky enough, we carry a sense of the future and how we expected it to be. We planned our finance, our holidays, our way of loving, living and dying. All of that is impacted on by the coronavirus and any plague. We have had to learn how to be separate from our children, our partners, our friends and family. We give birth in isolation and we die in isolation. We mourn in isolation.

The impact of this experience will take years to monitor and understand. Harlow *et al.* (1965) shocked the world half a century ago with their research on touch and communication in primates. Using methods of 'social distancing' and maternal deprivation, Harlow provided infant monkeys with the choice of a wire mother who had a bottle of real milk, or a cloth mother who provided softness but no milk. Infant monkeys spent significantly more time with the cloth mother, using the 'cold' mother only for quick feeds. With a cloth mother present, the infant could face impingements, but without a cloth mother, the infant would show signs of fear. Coming as it did in the midst of the 1960s' awareness of the needs of babies and children, this transformative paper aided major changes. Parents, who had been kept out of children's hospitals, were now allowed to stay with their children. This change did not come out of the air. It was in 1952, influenced by the work of John Bowlby, a giant in the field, that James and Joyce Robertson produced the film *A Two Year Old Goes To Hospital*. This film showed the emotional deterioration in a small child through being kept in hospital without an attachment figure. James Robertson (1911–88) was a social worker and psychoanalyst based at the Tavistock Clinic and Institute and his wife, Joyce Robertson (1919–2013), was an honorary child psychotherapist who worked at the Anna Freud Centre from 1956 to 1963, when she joined her husband to work at the Tavistock Institute on 'young children in brief separation'. Together they wrote books on the impact of separation (1971).

None of this, of course, would have been possible without the crucial work of John Bowlby (1907–90), the father of attachment theory. John Bowlby was a psychologist, psychiatrist and psychoanalyst, and he used the skills from all those professions in building up his pioneering body of work. From 1950 to 1990, he continued to research and educate on the seminal importance of attachment and attachment patterns in our species and the corrosive impact of separation from the main caregiver (Bowlby 1950, 1953, 1969, 1973, 1979a, 1979b, 1980). From an early age he was aware of his own personal loss when his beloved Nanny left when he was four, as well as the toxic impact on him of British boarding school at the age of seven.

Already by the start of the Second World War he became

concerned that young delinquents had experienced separation from a primary attachment figure in their first few years. Our forensic services have failed to implement his understanding. Rioting in prisons that is currently caused by restrictions on visits in time of plague and war shows us, only too painfully, the impact of separation to men in 'lockdown' for years. Additionally, we have seen in our child psychotherapy work the fatherless boys who long to become criminals in order to eventually meet their fathers in prison, or to know the 'home' their fathers lived in, which kept their fathers away from them.

If the giants in the field of touch and intimacy have worked so hard to help us understand the dangers of physical withdrawal, how will this be impacting on babies and toddlers who were infected or whose parents were infected? Will we see the three stages of protest, despair and detachment spread as quickly as the virus? How will this show in later life and how will this affect those whose homes are already unsafe or toxic?

How will our own attachment patterns affect how we navigate through these experiences or help others to?

Insecure attachments of avoidance and diffidence were needed to survive boarding school, being sent to the colonies and being in military service. Will our attachment patterns change now that such behaviours are admired and seen as needed? Since Covid-19, courageous individuals daring to name their non-binary sexuality publicly are no longer re-

6

warded in the same way in social media. When faced with a large threat, there is a fear of newness and accepting a widening of individual issues of identity. 'Why can't you be like Captain Tom?' is the question. Captain (now Sir) Tom Moore is the British man who, to mark his 100th birthday in April 2020, walked up and down in front of his house, raising money for the National Health Service. He raised over £30 million in this quiet, thoughtful way.

This book aims to provide information and ideas that will help us understand and address these questions. If we are secure enough in ourselves and our personal and professional identities, we will nevertheless still be facing major impingements in our lives. However, we will have an emotional compass to guide us. Whatever our personal psychological defences, they will have their gifts and their curses.

If we have been unlucky in our history, we may have nearly always had an idea that disasters could happen at any time. Now we might feel our view has been accepted and the world is an even more pessimistic place.

Pamela, a 45-year-old survivor of extreme abuse who also had to deal with cancer treatment, was more depressed than usual in a Facetime therapy session. 'I always felt I was contaminating and therapy was the world that told me I was not. But now the whole world is agreeing I am contaminating and must be locked away.'

Others with a significant trauma history can feel relieved that the rest of the world is openly expressing feelings that they have always carried in private.

Stefan, aged 36, commented, 'I don't feel mad at worrying every day about staying alive anymore. I can see that when faced with threat, normal people feel scared they will die, just like I do. And this time we are all feeling it at the same time.'

Suddenly we share the need to protect the one thing that most people cherish above all else – our lives.

EMOTIONAL FIRST AID BEFORE READING THE BOOK

1. Acknowledge that these are different times and that stress is almost inevitable.
2. Acknowledge how much our lives have changed.
3. Acknowledge that with a plague or war, we are facing the possibility or reality of death for ourselves or our loved ones.
4. Acknowledge that with a plague or war, we face the fear of contaminating or being contaminated.
5. Acknowledge that the only certainty is uncertainty but that we can do our best to achieve the best goals.
6. Acknowledge that cyber-intimacy is now going

to temporarily supplant physical intimacy.

7. Acknowledge that a percentage of those who have been unloved and deprived will not feel like protecting themselves or others.

8. Acknowledge that a percentage of those who have been unloved and deprived will want to feel immortal and immune to any danger.

9. Acknowledge gratitude for the freedom we have had to congregate, to shop, to walk and to visit for all the years up until now.

10. Acknowledge our need for physical movement, for affirmation of identity, for structured time.

11. Acknowledge the will for creativity and collaboration in much of the population.

The emotional maturity and creativity to deal with this new stage of national and local life will develop even more richly if we manage to openly acknowledge the difficulties posed first.

The capacity to reflect, write diaries, go online, learn a new language, learn a new hobby, be creative, tidy up, find physical activities, self-regulate or reach out to others can increase in a time where we have more time. There is also the capacity, as my daughter reminded me, for those who have been overworked, slaves of time, to let go of fixed structures. Who are we? What affirms our personal and professional identity?

The capacity to love is increased in a time where we are forced to realise the possibility of loss. At the same time, the increase in fear-driven violence is to be expected in those who cannot face this. Indeed, at this moment, calls to domestic abuse lines have dramatically risen and there are major concerns for vulnerable children and adults restricted to home where abuse occurs.

The capacity to be grateful to time is enhanced when we know we may not have more time. There is gratitude to those whose work allows us to survive in difficult times: hospital staff, delivery drivers, farmers, shopkeepers, care workers. At the same time, there is the increase in anger and impatience in those who feel in terror for their lives.

This means we need to find more ways, through technology, of providing physical and emotional support to those who require it.

What applies to the parent at home with the small child at one level applies to all of us. In order to make an emotional space for a baby and small child, the parent at home has to let go of their emotional control slightly and be more open to earlier emotional states, to lend themselves to the needs of a young age. To manage this well, the parent needs a partner, or neighbours or friends and family to provide emotional support. It takes a village to bring up a child. In the current situation there may be no-one who can safely enter the home; no-one to hug the parent, pick up the baby and give the parent a rest. Many parents cannot safely take their baby out in a pram, or their toddler to a playground, because of local risks.

The containment required through cyberspace and the creation of cyber villages is even more important at a time when trust in information and politics is low. Our regular television announcers, interviewers and newsreaders play a huge part here in containing us. For many of us, charging our phones and tablets is a crucial nightly containment ritual.

Unlike the Black Death, leprosy or actual visible warfare, we see little of the dying if they are not in our families or part of our professional work. We see momentary images on television screens of ventilators and people struggling to breathe but those we pass with careful social distance can be invisible carriers. They can be going about their normal day with nothing telling them they are carriers, spreaders. Others experience the virus as an ordinary cold. It is the invisible war that is so anxiety-creating.

Calling the NHS our frontline in this war carries a double-edged sword. Although our soldiers know their lives are in danger, they do not have the freedom to say no. In the words of Tennyson's *Charge of the Light Brigade* 'Theirs not to make reply, theirs not to reason why, theirs but to do and die'. However, doctors, nurses, ambulance drivers, bus drivers, shop assistants, refuse collectors, teachers etc., go to work to do their job and will not be hailed as a hero if they die. A strange dissociative game of Russian roulette began in which some considered it possible and acceptable for frontline workers to risk being killed doing their work. One of the issues this book examines, in Chapter 7, is the concept of moral injury where soldiers face committing acts that go against their whole moral compass. This is happening with our new civilian frontline.

An honest admission from political leaders that mistakes were made in the shock of the pandemic would have been accepted. However, disavowal, distortion and disinformation can all be symptoms of trauma. It has been moving so far to slowly witness a respect for scientists and technology in the face of unsuccessful populism.

Additionally, as such a plague has few barriers it means that everyone must face the reality of mortality.

Accepting the fact that we are all mortal is something unbearable for our species. This virus therefore makes us have to look death in the eye and realise we are on borrowed time. For those of us involved in trauma-informed care it is a chance to enrich ourselves and be enriched by those around us.

Plagues bring a chance to value other citizens whose

contribution can be ignored at other times. Taxi drivers and bus drivers face worse mortality risks than doctors and nurses. What about shop assistants and teachers? This is a philosophical moment to consider the value of every human life. Those with limited life conditions, those with intellectual and physical disabilities, those who are old, those who are in care homes – what is our worth? How much is there a eugenics-like death wish visible in the undercurrent? How do we titrate the psychological impact of loss of earnings versus the danger of early death? This is a chance for a rethinking of social values. How much, as a society, do we accept the psychic murder and premature death of those who cannot manage?

How we each reflect on these matters and contain ourselves is personal. Writing provides that space for me and here is a Covid poem I wrote.

Dot was safeguarded at home
Each morning her bruises opened
Like purple flowers

People have always
Washed their hands of her
*

This is the way we wash our hands

13

Wash our hands, wash our hands
*

'Poor little Coronavirus,'
Explained the tired mother,
Wiping her raw scrubbed hands,
'He's only looking for friends to join
But they don't want him'

'Just like me' says the child,
'Can I play with him?'
*

Jayden kissed his knife goodbye
Admired his face on its
Polished steel
He had a better weapon now
Easier to use and easy to kill

Put the knife back in the kitchen drawer
Goodbye to blood and DNA
Just a little cough, a little lethal cough
No Old Bill to frisk it away
*

Alf joked he'd bagged
A top university bird
Because she had a PPE
Social Distancing

Self-Isolation
He loved his new vocabulary
(Much snappier, he thought,
Than P and F and C)

*

Joe swaggered
Down the middle of the road
Pummelling his thin chest
Like a miniature Tarzan

Slow cars weaved fearfully around him

'Go Jo', shouts Tequila Tamsin
'You're King of the Road'

*

Ed jumped Trace in the kitchen
'Now I'm shielding you'
He jangled the door keys
'Can't wait for lockdown!
What about a baby girl called
Quarantina?'

*

Coughing Colin
One foot in the coffin
Has never felt such joy
Wherever he goes

People disappear

'I wish I'd had this as a boy'
*

Clap hands for Mummy
Talk to her on the phone
She's looking after Nanna
In the old age home
*

Glorious Gabby
The selfie queen
Turns on the camera
In order to be seen

'I am no body'
She cries to the condomised computer
'I am nobody'
*

'I want to touch my fa-a-a-ace
I want to touch my face'
*

'You said I could only have my tablet
For one hour a day
And now you want me to do school on it all day'
Grumbled Ali
*

At midnight
Our Covid Cinderella
Walks to her hospital shift
It is no ball
She lacks a mask and gown
*

Mara the cleaner
Scrubs the Care Home floors
Sticky old crumbs of cake and jelly

Around her
Elegant politicians
soft-soaping their words
from the widescreen telly
*

Moira claps for the NHS
Each time she has her bath
'They helped me when I
Got the clap',
She laughs
*

How orphaned the country feels
How desolate it has been
Needing the brave over-90s
Captain Tom, Attenborough and the Queen
*

This is the way the world ends
My love and I with a boiled egg and slice of toast
And Waitrose unable to provide deliveries
And the earth and sea and sun and stars
And all the creatures therein
Just carrying on effortlessly
Without us

Valerie Sinason, May 2020, 'Bakings', *The Bakehouse Literary Magazine*

An overview

Humankind cannot bear very much reality.

T.S. Eliot, 'Burnt Norton', *The Four Quartets* (1943)

We are a vulnerable species. All humans experience a life that inherently involves external stressors that impinge on us. We face death, separation, loss, pain, anger, hunger, thirst, sexual angst, physical incapacity, mental incapacity. Millions of us face wars, dispossession, exile. This is before we consider the problems in Europe and areas of need in the UK.

In our current historical period, the International Rescue Committee (IRC) considers that a small number of countries, representing only six per cent of the world's population, have produced nearly 75% of the world's refugees (www.rescue-uk.org). More than half of the Central African Republic (2.6 million people) require assistance; 40 per cent of Somalians (over 4 million); 500,000 in Burkina Faso; 2.2 million refugees in Sudan; 2.5 million refugees from Afghanistan (with 9 million needing humanitarian assistance);

2 million displaced people from Nigeria; 5.7 million refugees from Syria, with 11 million needing humanitarian assistance; 5 million displaced people in the Congo, with 15.6 million suffering from food insecurity; and 3.6 million displaced people in the Yemen, with 24 million needing humanitarian aid. This is before we begin to look at the economic conflict and its damage in Venezuela or ongoing tragedies of dictatorships and sectarian struggles. How can we consider such numbers or understand them?

Under the euphemistic term 'immigration', so much a current part of political unrest in our small connected world, we see daily the impact of life on displaced people subject to wars, unrest, hunger, poverty, rape and torture. People like us. We also see daily the impact of life on poor, struggling communities who have to deal with further encroachment on the little they have. People like us. When safe, our identity changes and so we have the delusional hope that people going through such suffering are different to us, do not mind seeing their children die of starvation, do not mind having to make dangerous crossings over land and sea to try to reach a safer place, can cope with rape and stigma and starvation because of their geographical and ethnic background. This, of course, is social dissociation; the Marlovian defence of 'Besides 'twas another country and the wench is dead' (Christopher Marlowe, 1589). Confucius understood it even further back.

The flowers of the cherry tree
How they wave about!
It's not that I do not think of you
But your home is so far away.

Confucius commented: 'He did not really think of her. If he did, there is no such thing as being far away' (*The Analects*).

However, there is a limit to how much of the world's sufferings we can bear to see, hear or be truly emotionally present to. We all need to dissociate at times. Through my cyberspace post box, I hear from brave organisations, Amnesty, Reprieve, the innocent prisoners on death row, support needed for the tortured and displaced, fear of the coronavirus affecting refugee camps and prisons. How much can we hold?

As lucky-enough adults, we can experience pain for one child. Reading the diary of a 13-year-old Jewish girl, Anne Frank, written during the Holocaust in 1942, we can resonate with her experience. We can feel angst at seeing a photo of one baby or one toddler washed ashore with a dead parent from Syria or Afghanistan in the twenty-first century. We can feel the sadness of one frontline doctor or nurse being infected with Covid-19 virus but cannot cope with recognising the pain of all those thousands and millions worldwide who do not make it to safety. We can provide all our resources to one 'brave' survivor who makes the perilous crossing to somewhere that might be safer and use all our military resources to destroy the efforts of others to reach us. We call the person who reaches safety a hero or heroine, but when they are trying to reach us, they are an 'economic migrant' or something more toxic. We largely cannot bear to consider their plight. We need to denigrate their reasons for such dangerous travels in order to lessen our collective guilt at their deaths. When they die in transit, they are sanctified. They were not yet our responsibility. Or some of us feel it all too much, have been sensitised by our life experiences to feel more inter-connected to the pain of others. Either way, it can overwhelm us. Indeed, secondary traumatisation is understood as a consequence of getting close to people suffering something overwhelming.

Professionals working with trauma need to pay extra attention to self-care. Institutions can erect major psychological defences to avoid feeling the predicament of patients, and 'compassion fatigue' was a term created to describe the gradual erosion and lessening of compassion felt by frontline care workers for those in pain (Figley, 2002). Such processes lead to a double erosion of capacity. The well-known joke 'patients interrupt the smooth running of hospitals' illustrates the defences of excessive routine, some kinds of paper work and timed tasks when they are constructed to avoid emotional meaning. However, being a human container for the pain of the world is not viable either. Secondary traumatisation is where being exposed to the pain of another or others leads to symptoms of traumatic stress. Vicarious traumatisation is something that happens to therapists and counsellors due to the impact of the counter-transference. Many members of caring professions can be victims of over-dedication to duty. Opening up to more and more felt pain from others does not answer the problem. The problem is infinite.

Lewis Carroll understood this concept (see his poem 'The Walrus and the Carpenter', 1872) when his two characters, the Walrus and the Carpenter, feel overwhelmed by the amount of sand on the beach. They sadly reflected on the fact that the sand could never be swept away. Even if seven maids with seven mops swept it for half a year would they be able to sweep it clear? '"I doubt it," said the Carpenter and wept a bitter tear'. We are the resource when working with someone traumatised and it matters that we respect the needs of that rare resource – ourselves. We need to be self-ish to help others. The pejorative term 'selfish' is commonly understood but the importance of us paying attention to ourselves, to be truly self-ish in order to be able to be a resource for someone else, is often missed. 'Physician heal thyself' remains a universal and important tenet. Originally written in Latin, *'Medice cura te ipsum'* was a well-known proverb which Jesus quoted in Luke 4:23. Aeschylus, the legendary playwright of

Ancient Greece, allowed the Chorus to say to the tortured Prometheus, 'Like an unskilled doctor, fallen ill, you lose heart and cannot discover by which remedies to cure your own disease'.

Treatments that understand the relational equality between helper and helped (Howell, 2020) also help here by not expecting the person behind the couch or Skype or WhatsApp to be immune to human pain and infection. There is not an 'us' and 'them' but an 'us and us'. This is a rare time in which patients are aware that those who look after them physically/mentally/emotionally/spiritually are facing similar dangers and a similar reality, despite the many differences. Not having a garden or a balcony with outside space takes on a different disadvantage in a time like this.

As humans, we also express our pain to the extent, on the whole, that we feel services will contain us. It will be interesting to note what kind of accidents or injuries are minimised in the UK during the coronavirus lockdowns. In the so-called 'Winter of Discontent' in 1978–9, when James Callaghan was prime minister, there were widespread strikes, including one from ambulance drivers. In that period there was a major drop in drunken accidents.

A further crisis appearing also makes the previous problems smaller, and sometimes, just as with bodily torment, a larger physical pain makes the previous pain bearable. Indeed, in a time of civil unrest in Northern Ireland, the suicide rate went down when the external danger was high. You do not have to kill yourself when others wish to perform that task. In times of peace, there are many other problems. Against the tapestry of major suffering, what about the micro moments of painful experiences in everyday life in countries spared active warfare? The child who did not get placed in the football or hockey team? The baby crying at the absence in her mother's eyes? The teenager who did not get a Valentine's card or an invitation to the school dance? The child with a disability who is mocked? The teenager with a different colour/religion/ smell/sexual orientation or clothing to the rest of the street? Is that trauma? Being stigmatised for difference? The child or adult with a life-threatening illness? The daily drip feed of feeling unloved or stigma? The suicidal one? What about the adult who loses their job, their mind, their partner, their home? Is that trauma? Is being homeless a trauma? What about the drip feed of multiple impingements, cumulative trauma?

It was Masud Khan, the brilliant and troubled psycho-analyst, who delineated his concept of cumulative trauma in 1963. In a way this prefigured the adverse childhood experiences (ACEs), the seminal innovation in the 1980s, where the numbers of ACEs are shown to distinctively impact on adult mental and physical health outcomes. The ACEs also owe something of their moral heritage to the pioneer, Thomas Szasz. Szasz (1920–2012) was a psychiatrist and psychoanalyst born in Hungary and educated in the USA, where he was a professor of psychiatry. His powerful work (1961, 1970) spoke out against what he saw as the myth of mental illness, involuntary psychiatric treatment and advocated the right to be free from bodily and mental impingement by others. His stand for libertarianism is highly relevant in the field of trauma. This is because it not only applies to the trauma itself but to the secondary traumatisation that can come from unthought-through treatment.

He would certainly be shocked at the continued normalisation of physical violence towards children. This is a painful and complex subject. Although most citizens in most countries would agree that big people hurting little people is damaging, that percentage goes down when governments debate the right of children to grow up without the fear of corporal punishment, attacks to their body in the name of 'reasonable chastisement'. There is a wish to make a major discrimination between hitting children for punishment and physical abuse. Sometimes, of course, a worn-out parent gives up on reason when all other methods to curb an undesirable behaviour have failed and hits a child, despite knowing it provides a moment's peace but then causes more problems. Afterwards, such a parent usually feels guilty at not managing the situation. Some countries in Scandinavia made hitting children illegal before the rest of the world, were able to aid such parents by devoting resources to finding other ways.

On one trip to Sweden with my daughter nearly 30 years ago, we went to the largest funfair in the country – the Liseberg amusement park in Gothenburg. There was all the noise of a fair, music, shouting, tired children, excited children. I suddenly stopped still. Something was missing. To my shock I suddenly realised what it was. Every fair in England that I had ever visited included in its tapestry of colour and noise the sound of children crying because a tired parent had hit them. Here, in Sweden, with all the familiar sights of both happy children and tired children wanting one more go, one more expensive ride and tired-out parents, there was something missing – no-one was hit; no-one was crying for being hit. I felt like a visitor from a primitive country.

We look with shock at the way Victorian children could be flogged, but closer in time, the way children could be hit with implements like canes or straps in schools up until 1986 is still too close for comfort. However, any attempt to ban such practice in the home has still failed in twenty-first-century England. Scotland has become the first country in the UK to make it a criminal offence to assault children, providing the same protection against physical actions that adults receive.

How then will we look back at the enormity of adults

almost all over the world fighting for a right to inflict pain on a child in their own home, in what should be their safest place, in our time? What does it mean about our attitudes to children or our unconscious responses to our own up-bringings that interpersonal violence to adults is illegal but not to children?

Where a child fears attacks on his or her bodily autonomy from attachment figures, how does that impact on further external trauma? Despite the endless research showing how violence breeds violence, we have failed to end this process. Love, loyalty and attachments to parents and past teachers can make it difficult to explore this. It can also be harder for some children to speak of sexual abuse when close adults are legally allowed to hit their bare bottoms. Indeed, there is a link between the two subjects.

Where does sexual abuse as a trauma fit in? Is the use of the term 'abuse' a linguistic denial of trauma? Abuse is some-times treated as if it was a medical condition with symptoms. Indeed, as McQueen *et al.* comment (2008), 'child abuse, whether it is sexual, physical or emotional abuse, or neglect, are experiences, not clinical conditions' (p.11). Why do we use the word 'abuse' instead of 'rape' and 'torture'? Only one in 65 rape cases reported to the police results in suspects being summonsed or charged (the *Guardian* analysis, 26 July 2019). Four years ago, the figure was 14 per cent and now it has dropped to 1.5 per cent. The decline in rape prosecutions is even more concerning at the time of #metoo, when victims around the world were starting to report more attacks. There appears to be a wish to not know the reason for this disturbing decline.

It was John Bowlby (1979a) who wrote the transformative paper on 'Knowing what you are not supposed to know'. In every family, country, group, there is something that we pick up unconsciously as forbidden knowledge. It stays dissociated from, disavowed in a special mental 'oubliette' (from the French 'to forget' (*oublier*)). The French had a particularly awful dungeon underground in which prisoners were fed occasionally through bars at the top or forgotten. We have pockets of such unwanted memories.

In the UK, 20 to 30 per cent of girls and 10 to 15 per cent of boys are abused (McQueen *et al.*, 2008). A conservative estimate is that 11 million citizens in our UK population have been abused. When we know that childhood abuse leads to almost every physical and mental health problem possible, we are looking at an invisible epidemic we cannot bear, and that is much larger than the coronavirus.

Indeed, it is a sign of a working democracy that the BBC and other major television and radio providers have reported on the increase in helpline calls concerning domestic abuse and assault during lockdown. On 6 April 2020, the charity

Refuge reported a 150 per cent increase in helpline calls and an estimated 25 per cent increase in abuse. Lockdown and quarantining mean a worrying number of children and adults are at the mercy of their abusers, with no respite. Additionally, those who are both victims and perpetrators are deprived of their access to help in this period, lessening their capacity for self-regulation. Of greater concern is the possible homicide rate to consider against the deaths from the coronavirus.

In July 2019, a 51-year-old man from England, Carl Beech, was jailed for 18 years, longer than for many murderers. His crime was to be a 'fantasist'. In usual circumstances, we understand the psychological problems of liars or fantasists. This is a very small problem among all the mental health problems that exist. He stated he had been abused in the 1970s and 1980s by famous politicians and senior members of military and security services. It seems possible he had stolen other people's accounts. However, the powerful retaliatory wish to silence a disturbed man who said there was a VIP ring at Westminster, in the heart of Parliament, meant he received a savage retaliatory sentence for saying what other survivors have said. A fantasist can speak someone else's truth. In silencing him, countless others now cannot speak. To be wrongly named is to be abused and it is remarkable that wrong accusations are so rare. However rare, no-one would wish anyone to be wrongly accused of such heinous crimes. However, the reputations of millions of survivors whose cases never reach court have been deemed less important than a savage sentence to correct the slanderous comments made about a handful of well-known figures. Frontline professionals supporting the one in four people who have been abused face attacks to their reputations daily. The disproportion of the response to Carl Beech raises almost as many questions as his alleged lies do.

Reading this book will provide you with the academic definitions needed to understand trauma and dissociation in general, it will also take you to the areas that are crucial but inadequately discussed. Hopefully it will do this in as undissociated a way as possible. Please take care of yourself while reading and note when you need a physical or mental break.

Although some are luckier than others, no age, religion, race or gender can avoid the pains of existence; and perhaps, for all of us, the deepest pain of existence, despite its enriching potential, is our knowledge of our mortality. Since we all share vulnerability and are 'the temporarily unimpaired', we clearly have social difficulty in accepting the ubiquity of trauma. We end up naming something difficult as a 'life event' when we have been unable to accept it as being part of the normal ups and downs of life. If all these downs were accepted as part of usual life, we would not have to call them 'life events'. They would automatically be that!

We will all die, and we will mourn the loss of others. Mortality, like coronavirus, is democratic in its reach. As Shakespeare (1623) expressed it, 'Golden lads and girls all must, as chimney sweepers, come to dust' (*Cymbeline*, Act IV, Scene 2). Through facing our mortality and our fear of loved ones dying, we develop a more robust response to trauma in ourselves and others.

3

What is trauma?

When we have a word for something, we can think we understand it. How do we find language for deepest loss, terror, fear and sadness? Can we? Are art, music, song, theatre and dance more equipped to reach that deep level? I provide two introductory quotations here. One is from a song, 'February' sung by the remarkable singer Joan Baez. Baez is an American singer–songwriter and activist whose work has always included songs of protest and social justice.

> *You stopped and pointed and you said*
> *'That's a crocus'*
> *And I said 'What's a crocus?' and you said*
> *'It's a flower'*
> *I tried to remember but I said*
> *'What's a flower?'*

'February', Joan Baez, 1997

You need to hear the beauty of her voice singing this song, but the words show the level of internal tragedy for people when objects lose their meaning and words are un-recognisable. A dismantling of the grammar of self is in operation.

The second quotation is a small extract from 'In the Middle of Life', a poem from the great Polish concentration camp poet, Tadeusz Rozewicz.

> *This is a table I said*
> *This is a table*
> *On the table there is bread a knife*
> *The knife is for cutting the bread*
> *Bread feeds people*

'In the Middle of Life', Tadeusz Rozewicz

He shows, like an ABC, how someone returning to the 'normal' world after traumatic catastrophe must start from the beginning again, testing the meaning of each word. How do you know a knife is for cutting bread when you have only seen it for cutting people? How do you know bread is for sharing if your tiny piece of crust has been stolen from you and is all you have to eat? How do you trust any word said by another? How do you sleep in a 'bedroom' when you were raped on your bed? How do you learn the word 'home' when your house is in rubble and there is no loving attachment figure near you?

I could have started with academic quotations, which will indeed come later. However, how differently would that have made you, the reader, feel?

I have begun with such quotations to ask us if we are partially dissociating when we try to write or speak academically about trauma and dissociation. The answer is that it is unavoidable. It is not only unavoidable, it is essential for our sanity. The issue is only a matter of degree.

Trauma comes from the Greek, meaning 'wound', from an earlier derivation meaning 'to pierce'. That is helpful as it underlines the fact that this is something that comes from the outside in. The term has long been used in a multi-layered way in medicine and surgery as meaning both the external, violent event that led to injury and the consequences to the organism as a whole. It is very important that it is acknowledged and understood as a two-part process – an actual moment of outside violence that has further internal repercussions. Indeed, in adopting that term, 'trauma', the helping professions largely accepted that there was an external stressor that comes suddenly and cannot be prepared for, that breaks through (pierces) the protective shield of skin and mind (and soul), and cannot be adequately processed.

However hostile the environment, it matters that the traumatic event is sudden. Something sudden cannot be prepared for. In our need for safety and agency, we can walk in a different direction if we are warned by sound or smell or touch that there is danger ahead. Although hurricanes can be sudden, in areas where there has been careful preparation and warnings on how to deal with them, there will be fewer traumas. This cushioning of traumatic repercussions where there is some warning is true for most external events (outside of war and atrocity), where it comes from a force of nature or an accident caused by humans, where everyone is taken by surprise.

I am emphasising the external here, which might sound surprising coming from a psychoanalyst. I am emphasising the external because all too often the brilliant light that psychoanalysis and psychotherapy can throw on the internal consequences of trauma, and on traumatic memory especially, get taken out of context and magnified in a way that can lead to the ubiquitous blaming of the victim. Needing to trauma-bond for survival to a violent parent or partner is an unsurprising consequence of some trauma, but it would not be there without the external trauma in relationships that caused such an attachment pattern.

INNOCENT TRAUMA AND BLAME

Natural disasters, which are large and public, are shared and are historical events. They are seen and accepted as fact and most people affected by them can feel 'innocent' or deserving of help; or these events are seen as innocent, unless people's religious beliefs see all natural disasters as caused by a deity or deities for punishment. (Indeed, even secular insurance companies do not insure against 'acts of God'.) Victims of accidents caused by human error (pilots/ship captains/builders), where the victims are ignorant of and not involved in the error made, also enter the category of 'innocent' victims. Charities find it easier to obtain money to help 'innocent' victims. However, personal man-made trauma, especially when involving emotional, physical and sexual rape and domestic abuse, is experienced as private and shameful. The victims blame themselves in an often life-long tragic pattern where an initial defence passes its sell-by date and becomes toxic.

The imprint of the Victorian concept of the 'deserving' and 'non-deserving' poor can be seen here. It is so hard to stay with the complexity of the whole. It is easier to divide people into deserving and non-deserving patients, deserving and non-deserving victims.

This division has entered the public debate on the National Health Service with deserving and non-deserving patients. All those whose need for food (too much or too little), drugs, alcohol, promiscuity comes from trauma-loading are seen through this non-compassionate lens as undeserving of medical or psychological help, and the moral cause of any consequent ill-health.

Shakespeare can always be relied on for understanding these processes and the projected hatred that goes to the stigmatised person. In the storm scene of *King Lear* (Act IV, Scene 6), Lear says:

> *Thou rascal beadle, hold thy bloody hand*
> *Why dost thou lash that whore?*
> *Strip thine own back*
> *Thou hotly lust to use her in that kind*
> *For which thou whipp'st her.*

And the victim is always ready to blame themselves too. Indeed, as we learn from Fairbairn (Sinason, 2014), blaming yourself as a victim is a key defence that, in the end, causes more damage than protection. 'If I had not gone out that morning', 'If I had only made a phone call before', 'If I had been good enough', and perhaps, deeper than anything else, 'If I had not been tainted with the me-ness of me', then this would never have happened. The poet Gerard Manley Hopkins understood this in one of his despair sonnets – 'God's most deep decree bitter would have me taste. My taste was me' (1885). Fairbairn called this 'the moral defence' (1952). Ferenczi (1929) took this further in understanding how, at the extremes, an unwanted child could pick up the hostility of the environment and enact it by dying. Bowlby and Winnicott were the giants. showing us how the external environment that we breathe in is the primary actor which then activates our internal unconscious responses.

The reflective position is also, 'There but for the grace of God go I'. This has been attributed to John Bradford (1510–55) who was burned at the stake for alleged crimes against Mary Tudor. '... on seeing evil-doers taken to the place of execution, he was wont to exclaim, "but for the grace of God there goes John Bradford"' (*Oxford Dictionary of National Biography*, Stephen (ed.), 1886).

Staying compassionate and non-judgemental in the face of trauma is crucial in this work. However, we need to be well resourced to maintain a reflective position at such times and that includes the basic understanding of how we respond as a species.

As a species, we do not have many alternatives when faced with trauma. In 1915, Walter Cannon, a professor at Harvard Medical School, coined the term 'fight or flight' to describe an animal's response to threat. What he learned was put into a popular later book in 1932 *Wisdom of the Body*.

The instinctive animal responses of flight, fight, freeze are physiological, immediate responses to danger or perceived danger. The responses accelerate heartbeat and lung action, constrict blood vessels, liberate fat and glycogen, inhibit the lacrimal gland and saliva, create tunnel vision and other features. This gives the body increased strength and energy in external situations. This was seen to be an essential feature of the later term 'PTSD' and hyperarousal. During Cannon's time it was, of course, seen as 'shellshock'.

However, when a child faces near-death experiences regularly at home, it wears down their defences, and affects the prefrontal cortex. The non-stop emergency alert means there is less energy for the usual developmental, social and intellectual tasks, leading to learning problems as well. Many distinguished clinicians and researchers have worked on this, including Van der Kolk and Greenberg (1987), Van der Kolk (2015), Perry (1994), Rothschild (2000, 2011) and Schore (2003, 2019).

Luckily, a small child or vulnerable adult has one other potential answer in their unconscious survival tool-kit: dissociation.

Dissociation, at the extreme level, is a small traumatised child or exhausted vulnerable adult who cannot manage the instinctive animal survival responses of flight, fight or freeze.

He or she is too little/weak/traumatised to run away from

an abusive adult or adults so ordinary flight is impossible.

He or she is too little/ weak/traumatised to fight a big person or people so fight is impossible as a defence.

He or she would be in other danger through freezing.

With no fight, flight or freeze for defence, and having to face 'fright without solution' (Hesse and Main, 1999), the creative child can run into another part of their mind. But there is a cost to this brave act of liberation.

Marcus Aurelius, the 'philosopher' Emperor of Rome nearly two thousand years ago, understood how dissociation was needed (Marcus Aurelius, 1964).

Unbearable pain carries us off; chronic pain can be borne. The mind preserves its own serenity by withdrawal, and the directing reason is not impaired by pain. It is for the parts injured by the pain to protest if they can.

All these centuries later our professionals still find it hard to allow those injured parts to protest. Whatever virtue signalling we go in for in different decades, we do not want to hear how grievance comes from grief. We prefer to denounce the 'trouble makers' in Black Lives Matter protests, trans action groups, gay rights or disturbed, deprived white groups, rather than see where the pain is. Hopefully, this book will aid the process of taking those other voices on board.

A bunch of fives: A mathematical trauma education!

This section provides a gathering of themes that happen to come in fives. This makes them easy to understand and learn from. Perhaps because we have five fingers on each hand and five toes on each foot, it is easy for us to observe processes in fives! I also like the fact that, from the early nineteenth century, a 'bunch of fives' was a boxing image, meaning a fist.

It was Charcot who pointed out the need for a victim to complete an action, so here is an action on behalf of those who do not always speak, over concepts that could help.

They do not have to all be read in a row. You might prefer to dip in and out, see which ones you are already familiar with or which might cause further reflection.

THE FIVE COMPONENTS OF HUMAN RIGHTS INFORMED THERAPY

Let us start with the optimum shared culture in which we can place our thinking – human rights. The five necessary components for a treatment to adhere to basic issues of human rights make up the name FREDA.

1. **F**airness
2. **R**espect
3. **E**quality
4. **D**ignity
5. **A**cceptance.

Increasingly, professionals working with stigmatised groups are appreciating the importance of a human rights lens with which to evaluate their work. Those with an intellectual disability, for example, are rarely receiving these five crucial ingredients for a relationship that ensures growth.

> *Susan expressed concern that in her long-stay hospital ward there was no private shower. The small number of showers available for the large group of women did not have curtains. In a therapy group we asked the questions: Was this fair, did it show respect, equality, did it provide dignity and acceptance? The answer to all was a resounding 'no'.*

When working with stigmatised minorities, former political prisoners, refugees and torture victims, using the lens of FREDA is particularly helpful.

SINASON'S MNEMONIC:
MAD, BAD, SAD, SICK, SUCK

Here are five alternative paths that can be taken. There are not many. Our heredity, environment, constitution make us more likely to gravitate to one path rather than another, but they encompass our possibilities.

1. Go mad – and you get psychiatric services.
2. Go bad, criminal – and you get forensic services.
3. Go sad, depressed – and you get medication, even though maybe therapy is best.
4. Go sick, somatise – and you get medical treatment.
5. Go suck, addiction problems, drugs, drink, food, sex, relationships – and you get addiction services.

All that has happened is that we are hurt, overwhelmed with something, and yet completely fragmented services spring up that do not want to see the common aetiology. Each 'choice' of symptoms provides a different group of professionals. The range of language, treatment and practice of these different professionals can be enormous. Understanding that these multiple professional groups with their different language and treatment protocols are only there to respond to the same single issue: hurt. Hurt allows there to be a less shaming attitude to mental health. Hopefully it will also lead to a unified umbrella of theory. However, trauma-informed treatment is still too rare. We hope that reading this book will help to increase the numbers of trauma-informed therapists.

John Read (2010) and others (Larkin and Read, 2008) shocked the academic establishment through academic papers showing how many mental health labels came from trauma. Validating the work of trauma-informed therapists, they found sexual abuse, for example, a core cause of psychosis. This is not new. Szasz had worked with this half a century earlier. However, within our lifetime, conservatism in the health service found it easier to almost blame the patient for their illness rather than understand its aetiology.

Daniel Defoe (1711) understood that:

I tell you gentlemen, in your poverty, the best of
you will rob your neighbour; nay, go further, as I
said once on the like occasion, you will not only rob
your neighbour, but if in distress you will EAT your
neighbour, ay and say grave to your meat too –
distress removes from the soul, all relation, affection,
sense of justice and all the obligations, either moral

or religious, that secure one man against another.
Not that I say or suggest the distress makes violence
lawful; but I say it is a trial beyond the ordinary
powers of human nature to withstand.

These external impingements that lead to traumatic responses are also exemplified by adverse childhood experiences.

Adverse childhood experiences are a way of documenting traumatic events in childhood and up to the age of 18. The actual number of adverse circumstances significantly relates to negative outcomes in adulthood. Felitti *et al.* (1998), the creator of the adverse childhood experiences questionnaire, found that the actual number of adverse circumstances people experience significantly and directly relates to negative physical and mental health in adulthood. He began this work in the mid-1980s and continued into his 80s. The larger the number of adverse experiences, the higher the risk of social, economic, physical and psychological problems.

PETRUSKA CLARKSON (1995): THE FIVE DIFFERENT KINDS OF THERAPEUTIC RELATIONSHIP

Professor Petruska Clarkson (1947–2006) was a South-African-born psychologist and psychotherapist who came to the UK and co-founded the training school, Metanoia.

Professor Clarkson set out five different kinds of therapeutic relationship:

1. The working alliance. This is the relationship between a professional and a client/patient.
2. The transferential countertransferential relationship. This refers to the unconscious and conscious feelings that are transferred during treatment.
3. The reparative/developmentally needed relationship. The attuned therapist might also be making up for gaps and hurdles in the developmental history of the client.
4. The person-to-person relationship. A real human connection between two citizens who happen to be a helper and a client.
5. The transpersonal relationship is the real, authentic concern and connection for the inner life of another.

CAROLYN SPRING'S FIVE FS

Carolyn Spring is a survivor of dissociative identity disorder (DID) who founded PODS (Positive Outcomes for Dissociative Survivors), one of the key UK training and support organisations in dissociation and dissociative identity disorder.

Carolyn Spring (2012) looks at five Fs to help with thinking about dissociation.

1. Friend: the first attachment figure.
2. Fight: this is an acute stress response described by Walter Cannon (1915, 1932), who showed that, like other animals, there is a physiological response to an actual threat or perceived threat.
3. Flight: this is also an acute stress response described by Walter Cannon (1915, 1932), who showed that, like other animals, there is a physiological response to an actual threat or perceived threat.
4. Freeze: this is where, if we cannot find security or fight or run, our bodies find a way of freezing.
5. Flop: 'This is a state of total submission when all the muscles go floppy and both the body and mind become malleable.'

Carolyn Spring has spent years educating the professions and survivors on how to understand these issues. Although her first four categories are shared widely and understood, her fifth includes the awful 'flop', where someone is reduced to be a puppet on a string. She looks at the ways a child responds to danger. First, there is a wish for a 'friend', an attachment figure. If that does not work, there is an angry need to 'fight'. If that fails, there is 'freeze', a paralysed state. However, she sees 'flop' as a state of total submission. Higher functioning of the mind is not available in such a state, as this is a 'zombie like' state in which there is no protest.

Zombies are known in contemporary culture as something from a novel or film about the undead, in which a corpse is reanimated. However, under the torture inflicted by Francois 'Papa Doc' Duvalier in the 1970s in Haiti, his particular special operations unit, the Tonton Macoute, were also known as zombies. The term Tonton Macoute meant an uncle (Tonton) who kidnaps children by snaring them in a sack (Macoute) and carrying them off to be eaten. The deprivation in the Haitian community and the level of violence meant that such iconic terms had powerful literal meaning. Tragically, the experience of children and adults who have been trafficked or assaulted, raped and tortured in organised ritualistic groups represent this state of flop: total abject submission. During the Holocaust, the term '*Muselmann*' was used to note those who were the walking dead, skeletal and resigned to death. They showed no responsiveness to what was happening around them. This German word has a further painful origin, meaning Muslim.

Primo Levi (1987) described them:

*Their life is short but their number is endless;
they, the* Muselmänner, *the drowned, form the
backbone of the camp, an anonymous mass,
continually renewed and always identical, of
non-men who march and labour in silence, the
divine spark dead within them, already too empty
to really suffer. One hesitates to call them living:
one hesitates to call their death, death, in the face
of which they have no fear as they are too tired to
understand.*

THE FIVE STAGES OF STRESS

Trauma affects our entire system, mind and body.

1. Alarm: fight–flight in which adrenaline pulses through your body ready for any action needed.
2. Resistance/damage control: the body attempts to recover from alarm but, if the core problem is not dealt with, more stress goes to the body.
3. Recovery: self-regulation and relaxation.
4. Adaption: you accept stress as part of daily life and it builds up, adding to ill-health.
5. Exhaustion/Burn out: if stress becomes chronic, somatic problems increase.

Mary faced domestic abuse (assault in the home) on a daily level. The impact of going through all these cycles on a daily level is toxic. Unsurprisingly, Mary has a range of problems that come from the breakdown of the autoimmune system.

Perry (1994) is just one of the eminent researchers who have shown that ongoing trauma can lead to irreversible neurobiological change.

Jonathon, aged ten, fell off his bike. He was badly bruised as a result of it. Nevertheless, with supportive family, he went through the first three stages very quickly, leading to greater resilience in readiness for any further such incident.

THE FIVE STAGES OF GRIEF

From Kubler-Ross (1969):
1. Denial: a refusal to accept the death of the other.
2. Anger: anger with life, with a deity, with medicine, that the other has died.
3. Bargaining: pleas to deities, a focus on all the 'what ifs'.

4. Depression: the sense of loss finally breaks through.
5. Acceptance: loss remains but grief has been processed.

These famous five stages have been crucial in aiding bereaved children and adults, but it is important to note they were not intended to be a rigid list or progression. Grief is not linear.

These famous five stages have been crucial in aiding bereaved children and adults.

INTENTIONALITY AND THE FIVE BASIC PARAMETERS

Pynoos and Naker (1988, 1993) found there were five basic parameters for an internal traumatic event.

1. Proximity to the violence
2. Lethality of the instrument
3. Intentionality
4. Object of the violence
5. Seriousness of the injury.

This seminal work linked together a further five factors which overlap with the ones already provided. Proximity to the violence can mean geographically in terms of explosions, warfare, floods, but also emotionally closer in terms of the perpetrator being an attachment figure. There will be more on attachment figures later.

Without support or constitutional robustness, this initial wound can be frozen or fossilised, forbidding any renewal. Indeed, as early as 1893 in his work with Breuer, Freud saw the psychical trauma, or rather the memory of the trauma, 'as a foreign body which long after its entry must continue to be regarded as an agent that is still at work' (Freud 1893, SE3, pp. 27–39).

Psychoanalysis added further depth and complexity by showing how the external stressor could interact with the individual's internal world, including unconscious guilt and phantasy (Garland, 1991). It is indeed an enemy agent that was uninvited and which can take over the area it has entered as an alternative to freezing and compartmentalising. For example, a child could perceive an injury caused by a brick falling from a roof as an intentional punishment for feeling angry with a parent. Physical disability, intellectual disability and life-threatening physical illness (Hartman and Burgess, 1985) can have similar post-traumatic consequences to sexual abuse. This is important for hospital workers to know, as well as social workers and family members. The current emphasis on new papers can mean seminal work of just 40 years ago can be missed.

Alan

Alan, aged eight, with Down's syndrome, was referred for violent behaviour to male teachers and carers. He had turned his hurt at Down's syndrome outward, telling everyone, 'Daddy hates me. Gave me Down's syndrome.' His father had left home, not bearing the personal pain of a child with a disability. Alan perceived his Down's syndrome as an attack from his father. He saw himself as the object of the violence and he saw it as deeply intentional, lethal and deeply close.

Khalida

Khalida, aged eight, was injured by an explosion in Syria. She had a loving family despite the trauma they lived in. Although the explosion was nearly lethal and was close to her and caused serious injury, she did not see it as intentional. She suffered from post-traumatic stress disorder but her mental state was less traumatised than Alan.

Joshua

Joshua, a non-practising Jew, whose grandparents had died in concentration camps, was caught up in a riot in India where he barely survived. He

*said it had hardly affected him after the initial
shock because it was not aimed at him. 'It was
Hindus and Muslims, all Indian, and not against
me as a white Jew from England.'*

In later discussion, he said he kept repeating the words
from a Paul McCartney (1982) song 'Wanderlust': *'Captain
says they'll be a bust, This one's not for me'*. The fact that there
was no intentionality and that he was not the object of the
violence spared him the worst trauma. The proximity and
lethality were literally true but not symbolically. This is where
we need to respect and honour the inside and the outside.

JENNIFER FREYD'S DARVO: DENY, ATTACK, AND REVERSE VICTIM AND OFFENDER

Professor Jennifer Freyd of Oregon University coined this
helpful term to refer to a common reaction of perpetrators,
particularly sexual offenders, in response to being held ac-
countable for their behaviour. The perpetrator or offender
may **deny** the behaviour, **attack** the individual doing the
confronting, and **reverse** the roles of **victim** and **offender**,
such that the perpetrator assumes the victim role and turns
the true victim – or the whistle-blower – into an alleged

offender. This occurs, for instance, when a guilty perpetrator assumes the role of 'falsely accused' and attacks the accuser's credibility, and blames the accuser for being the perpetrator of a false accusation. We can see this in some of the negative responses to the Black Lives Matter movement.

Institutional DARVO occurs when the DARVO is committed by an institution (or with institutional complicity) such as when police charge rape victims with lying. (See Institutional betrayal in Chapter 8.)

FREUD'S FIVE PRIMARY ANXIETIES WHICH WEAVE INTERNAL AND EXTERNAL FACTORS

Anxiety is a key consequence of trauma and can refuel it. Reality anxiety is about actual real or potentially real events that cause anxiety. Freud (1926) saw it as ego-based. He saw neurotic anxiety as something coming from the unconscious and often linked to fear of punishment for speaking out. Moral anxiety came from the superego and involved fear of breaking a personal or religious moral code, leading to guilt and shame. However, his five primary anxieties encompass these:

1. The traumatic situation of birth
2. Loss of perception of the object (which is equated with loss of the object itself)

3. Loss of the object's love
4. Castration anxiety
5. Annihilation anxiety.

Garland (1998, p.16) considers Freud's concepts of five anxieties that are felt to be universal and potentially traumatic for all as crucial in modern understanding of trauma. She saw all these anxieties as having one key theme in common: 'they consist of the separation from, or the loss of, *anything that is felt to be essential to life*, including life itself. They therefore bring the individual closer to a psychic recognition of death'. Van Velsen (1997) points out that Freud's delineation of signal anxiety is also linked with the phenomenon of increased arousal in Post Traumatic Stress Disorder (PTSD) (p.61).

If we bring back Alan's feelings that his Down's syndrome was caused by his father going away, we can see, using the lens of Freud's five anxieties, how this model also helps us understand Alan's predicament. Alan's birth was traumatic, with his disability not being accepted, he lost his father and his father's love, feared punishment and death from his father.

THE FIVE THEMES OF THERAPY IN WORK WITH INTELLECTUAL DISABILITY

These themes (Hollins and Sinason, 2000; Sinason, 2002) are trauma based and add to the vulnerability to trauma of people with an intellectual disability. They fit remarkably the template of Freud's primary anxieties. Dr Valerie Sinason and Baroness Sheila Professor Hollins came to these points in parallel and then combined them.

1. The fact of the disability itself (including the conscious and unconscious fantasies that accompany it).
2. Loss of the normal self who would otherwise have been born, and to the family and community.
3. Sexuality – internally distorted due to the impact of the disability and the external attitudes.
4. Dependency – not being able to live autonomously.
5. Fear of death/murder – linked to the societal wish to eliminate disability.

A continued theme in work with intellectual disability is the experience of extreme annihilatory fear because it is hard (or impossible) for many to separate out the idea of amniocentesis, leading to voluntary termination of fetuses believed to be learning disabled, from a death wish towards children and adults with intellectual disability while they are alive. Dealing with an internalised death wish links with Kahr's work on infanticidal attachment (2007) that can be seen in adults with schizophrenia and Sach's (2017) development of this in terms of the aetiology of dissociative disorders. It is of interest how the five themes, drawn from years of clinical work, match the five primary anxieties.

For Freud, and later for his descendants, all these anxieties lead to not five, but ten defences. These are crucial for survival, however self-injurious they might appear.

1. **Denial**, a need to avoid reality.
2. **Displacement**, directing onto another and safer figure the anger you feel with someone else.
3. **Intellectualisation**, seeking quantitative facts rather than feelings.
4. **Projection**, misattributing uncomfortable feelings onto a particular person to avoid feeling them.
5. **Reaction-formation**, in order to hide an unbearable feeling, the opposite is espoused. For example, someone feeling shame could display exhibitionist features as a defence.
6. **Regression**, going back to an earlier stage of development.
7. **Repression**, an unconscious process of hiding

memories and thoughts that are disturbing.

8. **Sublimation**, redirecting thwarted or difficult sexual or aggressive feelings into sport, or useful physical activity or creative activity.

9. **Rationalisation**, assimilating fake information to try to make a case for a decision.

Unlike Jung and Charcot, Freud did not develop the concept of dissociation.

However, an updating of the important understanding of defence mechanisms would now include:

10. **Dissociation or compartmentalisation**, which involves the separation of normally related mental processes, leading in extreme cases to conditions such as dissociative identity disorder. Although everyone experiences dissociation in a different way, it involves a feeling of disconnection, which is a defence against mental pain.

FIVE SYMPTOMS OF DISSOCIATION

Dr Marlene Steinberg (1994a, 1994b, 1995; Steinberg and Schnall, 2000), an American researcher and psychiatrist, researched the key diagnostic test that allows accurate pinpointing of dissociative disorders.

The SCID-D (structured interview for the assessment of DSM dissociative disorders) can evaluate whether a person is experiencing specific dissociative symptoms and whether these symptoms are interfering with their relationships or work and whether the symptoms are causing distress.

The five symptoms of dissociation include:

1.   **Amnesia** or memory problems involving difficulty recalling personal information.

John

John, aged 55, had no memory of his life from eleven to eighteen. Otherwise he functioned well. After being diagnosed with amnesia, he entered into therapy where it slowly emerged that he was abused and bullied throughout his secondary school life. In treatment, he remembered a time where he ran away from school and ended up in a part of the country he did not know and with no awareness of his name or address. This was an amnesic fugue.

2.   **Depersonalisation** or a sense of detachment or disconnection from one's self. A common feeling linked to depersonalisation is feeling like a stranger to one's bodily self.

Susan

Susan, aged seven, had an out-of-body experience when assaulted by her mother. She could see herself looking down from a great height. In a swimming lesson at her primary school, she told her teacher she did not know where her arms were to make them move.

3. **Derealisation** or a sense of disconnection from familiar people or one's surroundings.

Steve

After losing his job and having to clear his desk at work, Steve felt the walls and ceiling were spinning. He still felt he was in his body despite his emotional hurt but the environment was abnormal.

4. **Identity confusion** or inner struggle about one's sense of self/identity.

Sam

Standing outside a public toilet, Sam, aged 22, did not know if he was male or female and which toilet to go into. Despite having an arts degree, he also had no idea what job he could or should apply for.

5. **Identity alteration** or a sense of acting like a different person.

Joanna
Joanna moved from being angry and loud to someone with a quiet voice and manner. She could hear the change in her voice and manner but had no control over it.

Dissociative identity disorder, the extreme point on the spectrum of dissociation, has a primary requisite of a disorganised attachment as well as trauma. Therefore, attachment theory is crucial to work with trauma.

THE FIVE ATTACHMENT PATTERNS

These come from Ainsworth's development of the work of John Bowlby. They will be explored further in the chapter on dissociative identity disorder.

To research attachment styles, Ainsworth and Wittig (1969, pp. 71, 78) developed a technique called the 'strange situation classification' (SSC). Infants aged between 12 and 18 months are placed for a minute with an experimenter. Then parent and baby are left alone. Then a stranger joins parent and baby. Parent leaves and infant is left alone. Stranger returns and then parent returns and stranger leaves. An observer watching through a one-way screen can note proximity and contact-seeking, exploring behaviour, avoidance and resistance to contact. From this it could be seen that:

1. **A secure baby (type B)** can explore and play while the caregiver is present in the room, using him or her as a secure base. The child will also be able to engage with the stranger when the caregiver is present. The child is distressed by separation, seeks caregiver on return, is easily reassured and returns to play. The caregiver is sensitive and responsive.

Two other forms of attachment were noted that were each considered a different example of insecure attachment. I have taken a mathematical liberty in giving them a separate number each when they were seen as parts:

2. **Insecure avoidant (type A)** The child with an insecure avoidant attachment (the famous British 'stiff upper lip') does not show distress at separation and does not seek mother on return. However, there is a high level of body stress under the apparent calm. Caregiver is either dismissive or interfering.
3. **Insecure anxious/ambivalent (type C)** The

child with an anxious ambivalent insecure attachment shows distress before separation and is clingy and difficult to comfort on primary caregiver's return. The caregiver is insensitive and unpredictable.

However, there was a more distressing group of children who could not be coded into the patterns above and Ainsworth (1964) saw these as disorganised disorientated.

4. **Disorganised disorientated** They showed grossly disorganised behaviour, were apprehensive in the presence of their parent and the parent appears frightened or frightening.

The term 'disorganised' was used as the emotions experienced by the child disrupted its attachment system, often generated by fear. Contradictory behaviours, spinning, moving towards the caregiver and then away, or freezing and dissociation are just some of the responses. Liotti (1992) was one of the first to apply the knowledge and predictions from attachment patterns to the field of dissociative disorders.

In other words, we had secure attachment and now three different kinds of insecure attachment.

However, in the field of dissociative disorders, a further subsection of D babies has been named 'Double D babies'.

5. **'Double D babies' and the infanticidal attachment** (Richard Bowlby, 2006, personal communication) and the nature of their attachment has been termed 'infanticidal attachment' (Kahr, 1993, 2007; Sachs, 2017, 2018; Sinason, 2017).

This last category is the attachment pattern that leads to the most severe dissociative disorder – dissociative identity disorder, what used to be called 'multiple personality disorder'. In this category, the child desperately tries to make sense of volatile, violent, fearful or fear-inducing behaviour in an attachment figure or figures. Pre-verbally, the child tries to respond to the alternate states of the parent. A nine-month-old baby, for example, crawled to her depressed mother to give her her own bottle of milk, but the moment the mother roused herself angrily, the baby froze.

(My daughter has suggested I could include among all attachment patterns the concept of a secure catastrophic attachment, in which a trauma inheritance from two loving parents could lead to a pragmatic awareness of the potential for danger at any time but from within a secure attachment! This has yet to be done!)

Each of these 'fives' merits discussion.

How do they impact on our past or present work and thinking?

How far do we feel our service has followed human rights' values? How far is there adequate equality?

Just the reading of these 'fives' on their own covers major areas of treatment and themes.

Definitions: Further definitions for curiosity and clarity

Definitions are a different way of thinking about trauma and dissociation. We can use our academic and logical minds. There are many high-level disagreements over what is included in international psychiatric definitions, as well as more subtle nuanced debates. However, we are not usually having to feel for the psychic pain of others so deeply when looking at these formal academic terms as when engaging with clinical meetings or writing. This list largely excludes the definitions that have already been provided.

Alter, alter-personality, others, self-state, part People with dissociative identity disorder (DID) use different names to describe their other selves and it is important to use their own language.

Among a younger generation of people with DID, we are now hearing terms such as 'Plurals'.

Borderline personality disorder (BPD) is a disorder of mood and how a person interacts with others. It's the most commonly recognised personality disorder. It includes emotional instability, disturbed patterns of thinking and perception, impulsive, intense but unstable relationships.

Complex PTSD (CPTSD) This presents in children and adults who have repeatedly experienced traumatic events such as violence, neglect and abuse, slavery, kidnapping, being a prisoner of war. It is usually more severe if the traumatic events happened in early life, if they were caused by attachment figures, had been endured for a long time alone and there was still contact with the person responsible. It can take years to be recognised.

Complex PTSD often involves suicidal thoughts, destructive behaviour, problems in relationships, somatic symptoms, inability to focus and concentrate, difficulty in controlling feelings, as well as the issues that occur with PTSD, such as negative thoughts about the world that grew after a trauma.

Mind, the mental health charity, uses definitions recommended by the NHS, add more empathic descriptions:

> *constant feelings of emptiness or hopelessness,*
> *often experiencing dissociative symptoms such as*
> *depersonalisation or derealisation, feeling as if*
> *you are permanently damaged or worthless.*

The National Institute for Health and Care Excellence (NICE) has not yet developed recommendations specifically for CPTSD. Additionally, lack of training can mean the overlapping features between borderline personality disorder and CPTSD are not understood. Although some people can be correctly diagnosed with both conditions, the more common problem is people being misdiagnosed with BPD.

Depersonalisation is the experience of feeling detached from your body, feeling that your body, arms or legs are distorted. Like Alice in Wonderland, you can feel smaller or larger.

Derealisation is where your environment does not feel real. Ceiling and walls might feel they are moving or blurred or sharper. The distance of objects in the room can feel distorted in shape or size.

Depersonalisation and derealisation can be disorders in their own separate right or they can combine into derealisation and depersonalisation disorder.

Dissociation is a mental state in which people feel disconnected from their sense of self, experience or history as a defence against stress. This can last for hours or days or continue, in more severe cases, for weeks and months. This can lead to depression and anxiety or, in more severe situations, can lead to depersonalisation and derealisation and finally to a dissociative disorder.

Dissociative amnesia is where someone loses memory or information about themselves, usually as a result of trauma. These memory gaps last longer than ordinary forgetfulness and are not the result of a medical condition. It is usually caused by trauma or stress.

Dissociative amnesia with fugue People can find themselves in unknown places with no idea of how or why they got there. It usually comes from overwhelming stress or trauma.

Dissociative disorders of movement and sensation involve seizures, loss of sensation and paralysis. This diagnosis can become confused with diagnoses of neurological disorders like epilepsy and strokes.

Dissociative identity disorder (DID) is not a personality disorder but a natural way of coping with an abnormal environment. It is the new term for multiple personality disorder. The *Diagnostic and Statistical Manual of Mental Disorders*, 5th edition (DSM-V) American Psychiatric Association, (2013) describes DID as including two or more distinct identities or personality states, each with its own relatively enduring pattern of perceiving, relating to, and thinking about the environment and self. A major improvement in DSM-V as opposed to DSM-IV is that a psychiatrist does not have to witness switching of parts/alters to make the diagnosis if the referring clinician, client or family members report it. An experience of possession can also be included in the diagnosis.

EPACE (enduring personality change after catastrophic experience) As put forward in the ICD-10 (*International Classification of Diseases*, 10th revision), EPACE can be caused by many consistent or repetitive traumas where escape is extremely hard or not possible (Brewin, 2019).

Other specified dissociative disorder (OSDD) means that the person has dissociative symptoms, but they do not quite accurately fit any of the other allied diagnoses. This can make it harder to gain treatment as, without specialist training, it might not be adequately noticed. However, it means the clinician will specify why this is the diagnosis.

Post-traumatic stress disorder (PTSD) is an anxiety disorder caused by distressing, frightening or very stressful events. PTSD can involve the person reliving the traumatic event through nightmares and flashbacks, and temporarily not realising it is not current reality. Not surprisingly this can lead to problems sleeping. There can be physical sensations of feeling sick, shaking, pain and sweating. There can be feelings of guilt and shame at the experience. It can lead to phobias, depression or anxiety, or drug and alcohol misuse. The hippocampus, responsible for memory and feeling, is also smaller in people with PTSD. Hyperarousal is possible due to high adrenaline levels. PTSD is experienced by soldiers who have engaged in direct combat, by firefighters (think of the experience of firefighters at Grenfell, the tragic London tower block fire), police officers, victims of physical and sexual abuse, assault and torture, the experience of losing a baby.

Although this is an accepted clinical condition and diagnosis, it is worth acknowledging that a senior police officer once referred to 'alleged PTSD', commenting that if the trauma has not been proven in court, it is alleged and therefore the condition is alleged. This illustrates the problems some survivors face with legal process.

PTSD was included in the *Diagnostic and Statistical Manual of Mental Disorders* of the American Psychiatric Association for adults in 1980 and for children in 1987.

PTSD was moved from the anxiety disorders category to a new diagnostic category: 'Trauma and stressor-related disorders'.

The 2013 *Diagnostic and Statistical Manual of Mental Disorders*, 5th edition (DSM-V, APA, 2013) took on more importance in the field of dissociation in that it included dissociation as a subtype of PTSD. Diagnostic criteria include a history of exposure to a traumatic event that includes symptoms from each of four symptom clusters: intrusion, avoidance, negative alterations in cognitions and mood, and alterations in arousal and reactivity. The sixth criterion concerns duration of symptoms; the seventh assesses functioning; and the eighth criterion clarifies symptoms as not attributable to a substance or co-occurring medical condition. Two specifications are noted, including delayed expression – in which full diagnostic criteria are not met until at least six months after the trauma(s), although onset of symptoms may occur immediately, and a dissociative subtype of PTSD – which is new to DSM-V. This includes depersonalisation and derealisation. In both specifications, the full diagnostic criteria for PTSD must be met for application to be warranted (DSM-V Criteria for PTSD, 2014).

The unexpected death of a family member or a close friend due to natural causes is no longer included, or that the response to trauma involved intense fear and horror. However, learning that traumatic events occurred to a close family member or friend does constitute a trauma.

Avoidance and numbing are separated into two different criteria. For the diagnosis of PTSD, one avoidance symptom is needed. Criterion D has been added – this is negative thoughts or feelings about the world that began or worsened after the trauma, and negative affect and trauma-related arousal and reactivity that began or worsened after the trauma.

Criterion D has been important in the forensic field in understanding reactivity that was caused by the trauma. It is also highly relevant in the field of intellectual disability where it is important to link the challenging behaviour to the preceding trauma. It is also relevant to behaviour after sexual assault.

PTSD in babies, children and young people Babies and under-fives who experience trauma can show signs of PTSD, even when pre-verbal. Wariness, anxiety, extreme clinginess, fear of sleeping, upsetting nocturnal awakenings, frozen numbness, loss of smiling and vocalising, regressing, more unsettled, high levels of distress on separation can be included here.

Children 5–12

Children are subject to the same traumatic events as adults. In addition, they can experience dangerous levels of bullying in their community, in school and on social media. They can show PTSD in different ways to adults. They might wet the bed, thumb suck.

For example, children might show PTSD in their play.

Jade

Jade (not her real name) lost friends and family members in the devastating fire in Grenfell Tower in London. At school, she continually role-played being a firefighter rescuing people from a fire. She drew the building on fire with people falling from the window all the time. She had a bottle of water next to her bed and became agitated if far from the bathroom.

Children 12–18

Teenagers are more likely to show impulsive and aggressive behaviours, sexual acting out and self-harm.

Quaternary structural dissociation (posited by Professor John Morton and Dr Valerie Sinason) is where the amnesia between different personality states, parts or alters is scientifically objective as well as subjective. While Professor Morton provided the tests to investigate the nature of their memory, Dr Sinason clinically noted there are narratives concerning installed DID, rather than DID as a spontaneous defence in such people. This does not mean they have suffered more or less, but it does mean the separate states need to be understood more.

Secondary structural dissociation is when multiple parts/personalities remain separate from the apparently normal part, which manages the daily functioning.

Secondary traumatic stress is what we experience when exposed to people who have been traumatised themselves, when we read or hear disturbing descriptions of traumatic events or witness acts of cruelty. Even professionals trained to manage situations that would be overwhelming for others can experience secondary traumatic stress. It is experienced by police officers, firefighters, clinicians, indeed anyone who is exposed to people who have been traumatised themselves, hearing disturbing descriptions of traumatic events or witnessing acts of cruelty.

Structural dissociation is a response to trauma and a disorganised attachment. The baby and small child cannot develop a coherent sense of identity and stays unintegrated. With one kind of trauma or a series of traumas, one part of the personality remains separate from the main personality. The separate part is known as the **EP, emotional personality**, and is often the child's personality. This is known as **primary structural dissociation**. The main part is known as the **ANP, apparently normal personality**.

Tertiary structural dissociation is dissociative identity disorder where there are both multiple emotional parts (usually with the child's memories) and multiple apparently normal parts (who manage daily life).

Trauma, at the deepest level, is exposure to actual or threatened death, serious injury or sexual violence through: (a) directly experiencing the event, (b) witnessing in person the event occurring to others, (c) learning that such an event happened to a close family member or friend, or (d) experiencing repeated or extreme exposure to aversive details of such events, such as with first responders. Actual or threatened death must have occurred in a violent or accidental manner and the experiencing is not through television, film or pictures unless work related. It is sudden and unprepared for and overwhelms.

Unspecified dissociative disorder (UDD) is a confusing category in that the former DDNOS (dissociative disorder not otherwise specified) has been divided into two categories, OSDD and UDD, in which symptoms bring distress and have dissociative features but not enough to fit a category. With OSDD, the clinician will say what the diagnosis is and, with UDD, they will not, because it is not possible or for other reasons. This is confusing but shows what a spectrum there is.

Dissociative identity disorder

DISORGANISED ATTACHMENT

The most extreme form of dissociation in response to trauma is dissociative identity disorder (DID). It largely comes from the painful double circumstances of both an external trauma and a disorganised attachment. Tragically, it is also the least understood and the least trained for. Indeed, its aetiology and symptoms have been disavowed and denied (Sinason, 2002, 2012), despite 90 per cent of patients meeting the criteria for DID reporting a history of physical and sexual abuse (Fonagy and Target, 1995).

Childhood attachment is a prerequisite to safety. Spitz (1945) showed how children in an orphanage who were physically cared for but who had no attachment figures were more vulnerable to dying. He also found that in an orphanage, despite impeccable hygiene, toddlers were more susceptible to illness and had higher mortality rates. Some of the traumatised, abandoned orphanage babes were given an optimum environment after 15 months, yet 'notwith-standing this improvement in environmental conditions, the process of deterioration has proved to be progressive. It would seem that the developmental imbalance caused by the environmental conditions during the children's first year produces a psychosomatic damage that cannot be repaired by normal measures' (Spitz, p. 25). Adults categorised as secure are significantly more likely to be securely attached adults (Waters *et al.*, 1995) and to have children attached to them (van IJendoorn, 1995).

It is thanks to the work of John Bowlby (1953, 1979a, 1979b) and its development by Mary Main (1977, 1979), Mary Ainsworth (1964) and Ainsworth and Bell (1970), and other colleagues that has led to attachment patterns being scientifically measurable across the world. Bowlby worked on the hypothesis that the nature of the relationship the child had with his or her primary caregivers would provide the basis for future relationships. John Bowlby wished to find a research base that could not be ignored as it was an established fact. Looking at how children dealt with separation, as in hospital stays, became a crucial base for exploration.

The strange situation was devised by Mary Ainsworth in the 1970s to observe and measure attachment relationships in babies aged between 9 and 18 months. The protocol of the 'strange situation' consists of a baby being observed in moments of separation and reunion. Parent and infant go into the room which is the research base and are initially alone. Stranger comes and talks to parent and approaches infant, and parent then noticeably leaves. Stranger responds to infant. Parent can watch in next room. Then the parent returns and greets the child and leaves again. This time the infant is left alone. Stranger comes in and responds to child. Parent returns and greets child and stranger leaves noticeably. The amount of exploration, level of stranger anxiety, response to loss with caregiver and reunion are all monitored. As well as secure attachment, there are those listed below.

I am repeating these categories that were discussed in Chapter 4 'A bunch of fives', as they are so crucial to how trauma is experienced.

We have a **secure baby** (B), and **insecure avoidant** (A) and **insecure anxious/ambivalent**(C). However, there was a more distressing group of children who could not be coded into the patterns above and Ainsworth (1990) and Main and Solomon (1990) saw these as **disorganised disorientated** (D). They were grossly disorganised in their behaviour, apprehensive in the presence of the caregiver, and the parent appears frightened or frightening.

The term 'disorganised' was used as the emotions experienced by the child disrupted his or her attachment system, often generated by fear. Contradictory behaviours, spinning, moving towards caregiver and then away, or freezing and dissociation are just some of the responses. Liotti (1992) was one of the first to apply the knowledge and predictions from attachment patterns to the field of dissociative disorders.

INFANTICIDAL ATTACHMENT

Indeed, in the field of dissociative disorders, a further subsection of D babies has been named 'double D babies', disorganised and dissociative (Richard Bowlby, 2006, personal communication).

The nature of their attachment has been linked to lethal attachment (Sinason, 1990) or internalised death wishes (Sinason, 1992) and then termed 'infanticidal attachment' (Kahr, 2007; Sachs, 2017, 2018; Sinason, 2017). Dissociative babies show such behaviours as clinging on for survival or dissociating or attachment trauma (Fonagy, 2006). If circumstances do not improve, the child grows up with the different states becoming more hard-wired and substantial. However, with treatment there is an excellent prognosis for children in safe homes to 'multigrate'.

When it comes to adults, there have been more years for the DID to embed itself. Relationships, work and leisure are already impacted on by it. Sometimes the abuse is ongoing, making it harder for change to happen as defences are needed to survive.

As the condition of DID is linked to family attachment patterns, it is not seen as an 'innocent' trauma. It evokes anxiety in professional networks. Additionally, it is seen as a forensic condition (Sachs and Galton, 2018) in that, whether by omission or commission, there is often a narrative around sexual abuse from an attachment figure (Fonagy and Target, 1995).

ORGANISED RITUAL ABUSE

Adding to the complexity of this condition, organised ritualistic abuse is frequently described as a key traumatic experience in those coming for treatment. All child and adult abuse linked to spiritual, religious or pseudo-religious beliefs evokes extra fear in the victims and, through them, to those they inform.

A working definition of ritual or ritualised abuse (Sinason and Aduale, 2008) is 'a child or adult is made to feel that they, their families or those they love are doomed in this life and in an afterlife if they do not obey what they are asked to say or do'. In other words, the attachment needs of the victims are used against them (Badouk Epstein *et al.*, 2011).

A fuller definition can be found on the webpage of

Professor Michael Salter (organisedabuse.com), to date the only criminologist worldwide specialising in research in organised abuse. He is a Scientia Fellow at the University of New South Wales and on the Board of the International Society for the Study of Trauma and Dissociation.

> *Ritual abuse refers to incidents of organised abuse that is structured in a ceremonial or ritualistic fashion, often incorporating religious or mythological iconography. Ritual abuse is a characteristic of particularly abusive groups and is typically associated with the torture of children and adults and the manufacture of child abuse material. Despite vocal scepticism about the existence of ritual abuse, it has been a feature of high-profile sexual abuse convictions in the United States and the United Kingdom. Professionals in a range of contexts continue to report encountering child and adult victims of ritual abuse.*

Therapeutic treatment of dissociative disorders is still in its infancy in the UK despite an increase in National Health Service concern.

As a survivor, Carole wrote (Sinason, 2012):

*No-one has been trained in this because if they
were, they would have to face our reality, our
torture, and it is much better to hate the victim or
lock them up and see them as abnormal than to
realise we are the shadow side of your normality.
Our normality is your worst nightmare. We live
your nightmare. What psychotherapy training
wants to hear about that? What historian of
theories cares about that?*

However, on the positive side, professional organisations supporting people with DID, such as the ESTD (European Society for the Study of Trauma and Dissociation), the ISSTD (International Society for the Study of Trauma and Dissociation) and RAINS (Ritual Abuse Information and Support) have been added to by organisations run by experts through lived experience and survivor professionals such as PODS (Positive Outcomes for Dissociative Survivors) and FPP (First Personal Plural). Additionally, the major umbrella organisations for survivors including Mind, Survivors Trust (with Fay Maxted as CEO) and NAPAC (National Association for People Abused in Childhood, founded by Peter Saunders), all include victims of organised abuse with DID in their remit.

To aid the therapeutic and scientific research, Brand and Brown (2016) were able to disprove the hypothesis that people with DID are fantasy-prone and/or suggestible and therefore in danger of espousing confabulated traumatic memories. Additionally, Simone Reinders *et al.* (2012) demonstrated that genuine and feigned DID can be reliably distinguished.

Treatment that demands integration is likely to fail as the crucial component in successful treatment is aiding democratic thinking. With many alters, or parts, in people with DID with many different hopes and aims, the hope is to provide a voice for all, to welcome and respect the role all have played, in helping to keep somebody alive. This means understanding so-called 'perpetrator' parts, who have survived by identifying with their abusers.

Mandy

When Mandy, aged 25, went to a therapist who was not trained in DID, she was traumatised by his approach. 'He said our aim was to get rid of all the others, children and mad ones who came out regularly, so that I could be there all the time. I told him that was what I used to think before I realised all the others were part of me and I would not be alive without them.'

The aim is merger, if it is possible, not murder!
Some will never be able to unite. The level of trauma used

to split them makes it unbearable or impossible to face all that trauma again by uniting. However, having a clearer narrative and learning how to share time allow more freedom. Readers can gain a sense of the lived experience of DID by reading books by survivors including *All of Me* by Kim Noble (2011), *Today I'm Alice* by Alice Jamieson (2009) or watching *May 33rd* (2004), a film written by Guy Hibbert, starring Lia Williams who was nominated for a BAFTA for her portrayal of a woman with DID. An introductory book for working with DID is *Attachment, Trauma and Multiplicity* (Sinason, 2011).

Despite all the work carried out in the UK, there are still limited professional clinical resources, but they include the Pottergate Clinic in Norfolk, directed by Remy Aquerone, and the Clinic for Dissociative Studies in London.

We now move from the trauma battlefield that rages inside the human mind, caused by external trauma, to war, the largest external trauma.

War and atrocity

Cry 'Havoc!' and let slip the dogs of war

Mark Antony, Act III, Scene 1, *Julius Caesar*

With such a condensed introduction to trauma, followed by definitions, let us use those tools to examine some of the traumatic impact caused by war.

All of us have been marked by war. Its impact passes down generationally. The impact of death, murder, injury, devastating sights and sounds, illness, rationing, separation, evacuation passes down through the generations. The small number of remaining survivors from the Second World War remind us of the impact on attachment patterns, eating habits that pass on for years.

War is inherently a stressor that is strong enough to break through the protective shield of mind and skin. With the human and largely male unwillingness to give up this form of behaviour, it continues worldwide.

History is largely the voice of the victor and, outside of profound acts of non-violence such as by Gandhi and Martin Luther King or hunger strikes, the male of our species especially has been involved in warfare. Female exceptions like Boudicca, or the mythical Amazon women who allegedly cut off a breast in order to shoot their arrows more lethally, are precisely that – exceptions. Indeed, the brilliant ancient playwright Aristophanes wrote a serious comedy which was performed in Athens in 411 BC, *Lysistrata*. It tells of a woman, Lysistrata, who persuades women of warring Greek cities to withhold all sexual contact from their husbands and lovers to enforce peace. Over two thousand years later we have still failed to understand how this gender division has persisted.

The mythical four horsemen of the apocalypse from the Book of Revelations in the Old Testament – war, hunger, plague and death – have always been understood, known and feared by our species. Unlike random acts of violence that meet with prison, violence conducted under the authority of the state is dissociatively perceived as normal. The abnormality of war is only understood by populations when in a reflective state of mind. Indeed, the increase of visual coverage of conflict areas, news, interviews, and the speed of feedback and social media that allow us to see the damage, aid our reflectiveness, especially when the war is not a popular one. This is despite the disinformation.

We keep learning to our cost that warfare is a time of enormous individual and group trauma, which impacts on generations to follow. Wars bring rape, famine, atrocities, slavery, physical wounds, and multiple deaths and losses. Wars destroy loving families, fathers, mothers, generations, and impinges on the minds of the orphaned and unloved. Unlike a popular war that can uphold some moral decisions, many wars evoke increasing ambivalence in democratic countries. This creates a bigger burden for the soldiers sent out on our behalf.

Nijenhuis (van der Hart *et al.*, 2006), in looking at how our minds structure dissociation, speaks of an 'emotional personality' (EP) who bears the pain of life while an 'apparently normal personality' (ANP) presses on. We could consider that a soldier from a lucky country is an EP, sent out on behalf of the rest of the country (which represents the ANP), to do battle, risk death and incur PTSD on our behalf, then that soldier returns and receives no heroic welcome because the war was unpopular. The emotional experience of a soldier returning from victory to a welcoming, cheering population makes a major difference to recovery. Think of the soldier returning to civilian life in the UK from Syria or Afghanistan with no welcome, struggling with flashbacks.

ABUSE, SUICIDE AND POSSIBLE MURDER OF RECRUITS

Training for war can be the start of the trauma for those who enlist. Within the UK (*Daily Mirror*, 2019), it was reported that at least 122 British army instructors have been court-martialled or disciplined in the last four years for sadistic 'hazing' ceremonies and recruit abuse. These facts came to public light after investigation into the deaths of four teenage recruits at the Princess Royal Barracks in Deepcut, Surrey between 1995 and 2002, amidst many claims of abuse.

Although the official verdict was that the soldiers had committed suicide, the concern from the press and families of army recruits led to questions in the House of Lords. In December 2004, military lawyer and QC, Nicholas Blake, conducted a major independent review. As well as many other points of concern, the review stated that a detrimental culture of bullying and unofficial punishments had grown. The Army Board of Inquiry, released two years late by the Ministry of Defence in 2009, supported the Blake Report findings and returned open verdicts on the death of the recruits.

While controversy remains over those open verdicts, on 18 July 2014, the High Court of Justice ordered a second inquest into the death of Private Cheryl James at Deepcut. The British fortnightly satirical magazine *Private Eye* (2015), in investigating the deaths at Deepcut, said there was material to suggest Cheryl had been the victim of serious harassment and sexual violence. She died in 1995 and it took twenty years to achieve a second inquest, in which there was a rare consensus in the British tabloids and broadsheet papers that there was a serious case to answer.

FEMALE SOLDIERS AND FEMALE RECRUITS

The Independent (Owen, 2016) highlighted a culture of cruelty 'where sexual assaults and rape were widespread'. These issues brought to the public eye the specific gendered experiences of female recruits and veterans.

Norway and Israel were the first countries to allow women to enter combat operations. In Norway in 2015, women were eligible for compulsory military service. In Israel fewer than 4 per cent of women were in combat duty in 2015. In the USA and Puerto Rico, there are approximately two million female veterans, approximately 9.5 per cent of the total population in 2015. In the UK, by July 2016, women were able to enter in close combat. Within the USA (Department of Defense Annual Report, 2019) there was an increase of sexual assaults reported on female service members aged 17–24. Among active duty women, 6.2 per cent experienced assault compared with 0.7 per cent of men. The survey results, as with Deepcut, found a positive correlation between unhealthy workplace climates and the risk of sexual assault.

Harel-Shalev and Daphna-Tekoah (2016; 2020), Daphna-Tekoah and Harel-Shalev (2017), Stachowitsch (2012a, 2012b, 2012c, 2013), and Shepherd (2008) are among the researchers looking at the particular issues women soldiers face in the military, both in training and in combat. They note the way women are seen as victims rather than as equal warriors alongside men.

Other issues involve what could be argued as 'false' promotion of female rights! It could be argued that the narrative of 'liberating oppressed women' in Muslim-majority societies (Sjoberg and Gentry, 2008) is potentially open to being exploited to legitimise the 'war on terror'. Indeed, it could be a cynical way to gain more female soldiers. Highlighting wars fought in misogynist countries could be inspiring, except when there is little evidence shown of aiding those groups.

Such false framings can in fact be detrimental to broader equality issues. It highlights women's status as weak victims, as well as claiming that they have universally shared peaceful interests. These ways of perceiving women follow a post-colonial script which depends on the 'other' being the violent one and associates women's equality only with western civilisation (Harrington, 2011, pp. 557–75).

There has been a more recent further issue that needs

mentioning regarding female soldiers. Extra tensions for military wives have been evoked over knowing their husbands are going to war in the company of other women. The sexual excitement that can be evoked as a defence against the aggression of war can lead to infidelity, which, in turn, can cause more emotional breakdown in the military. Same-sex partners have always had to deal with this.

RACE AND WARFARE

We can also examine levels of trauma according to race. Among Americans aged between 18 to 44 in the US Defence Department, 44 per cent are racial or ethnic minorities. Black people have consistently been over-represented among enlisted personnel (19 per cent in 2015) than commissioned officers (9 per cent).

In the UK, on 3 July 2019, law reporter Lucy Fisher wrote in *The Times* about two black paratroopers who were alleging that the British Army is 'systemically racist' and had failed to act when a spate of racial abuse was reported. They claimed targeted mistreatment from colleagues including racial slurs and swearwords. Private Hani Gue and Lance Corporal Nkululeko Zulu said that a picture of them was defaced by personnel with swastikas, Hitler moustaches and the caption 'f*** off'. Former colleagues were also said to have made offensive, racially themed remarks about groups in Kenya, and it was also said that a member of the 3rd Battalion, Parachute Regiment (3 PARA) had posted photos of paratroopers posing with Tommy Robinson, founder of the English Defence League, on their Facebook page. The English Defence League was founded in 2009 and presents itself as a single issue group opposed to Islamic extremism.

On 19 December 2019, Nicola Williams, the Services Complaints Ombudsman for the Armed Forces, called on the Ministry of Defence to tackle the increase in racism among service personnel. Indeed, on 7 January 2020, the *Guardian* reported that only 17 per cent of investigations returned guilty verdicts at court martials.

LGBT SOLDIERS

Across the world, LGBT recruits and soldiers are seriously bullied (Maresca, 2019). In South Korea, for example, sex between consenting men is allowed among civilians but not in the military. There is an atmosphere of mental and physical abuse that soldiers face under Article 92-6 of the country's Military Criminal Act (Amnesty International, 2019). The LGBT Military Personnel Index (Polchar *et al.*, 2014), brought out by the Hague Centre for Strategic Studies, offers one of the most thorough analyses here, including negating, from an evidenced perspective, the prejudiced basic assumptions that LGBT soldiers would not be equal to the task.

In 2019, a group of volunteer soldiers announced the first ever LGBT unit, The Queer Insurrection and Liberation Army, or TQILA, which is now fighting alongside Kurdish forces in Syria.

The new LGBT unit said it was driven to battle after seeing how ISIS targeted their community. 'The images of gay men being thrown off roofs and stoned to death by Daesh was something we could not idly watch,' they said (Lapin, 2017).

ISIS courts declared homosexuality a capital offence punishable by death. Since its rise in Iraq in 2014, the terrorist group released devastating anti-gay propaganda showing men accused of homosexuality blindfolded and being thrown off roofs in front of large crowds, and then stoned if they survived the fall.

The extra emotional experience of LGBT soldiers entering the double trauma of war and war with people who kill their own citizens for their sexual identity deserves serious attention.

CHILD SOLDIERS

Another category, which needs to be included separately, is child soldiers.

In 2017, it was considered that over 240 million children around the world were living in countries affected by conflict. Violence, hunger, rape and exploitation always occur in such traumatic circumstances. The main countries affected include the Congo, the Middle East, Afghanistan, Myanmar, Somalia, South Sudan, Sudan, Syria, Yemen, Nigeria and the Philippines. Almost half of the 881 child casualties in Nigeria resulted from suicide attacks and the use of children as human bombs. In areas of conflict, children are victimised not only by the trauma of war, loss, injury, separation from family or death of family, but also by being forcibly enlisted to carry out attacks on behalf of the ruling group.

Although the Secretary-General of the United Nations reminded authorities worldwide (United Nations, 2018) that children formerly associated with armed groups should be treated as victims, in various countries this is not upheld. For example, in Nigeria, over 1,900 former child soldiers, who had little choice in being made to join Boko Haram, a jihadist terror organisation, or whose parents joined Boko Haram, were deprived of their liberty. In Somalia, Al-Shabbab, a fundamentalist jihadist group based in East Africa, abducted over 1,600 children. Most of these were forcibly abducted and some 'joined', little knowing the abuse they were walking into.

Child soldiers, on being rescued, can, like raped women,

be blamed for their unchosen actions. Those who were forced to kill or injure their own families or neighbours have an extra problematic return. Many were drugged to encourage these behaviours or used as sex slaves.

Theresa Betancourt directs the Research Program on Children and Global Adversity at Harvard School of Public Health. She has shown how, despite appalling circumstances, children can become productive members of society, even in countries as under-resourced as Sierra Leone. In this country, 70 per cent had witnessed beatings or torture, 77 per cent had witnessed stabbings, hacking off of limbs, and shootings close up, and 27 per cent had killed or injured others. Since 2002 she has been tracking 500 children who were child soldiers in Sierra Leone. In treatment, they have nightmares, intrusive thoughts and violent images, especially those who had committed the most violence. Her group interventions aim to encourage resilience and minimise the most dangerous outcomes. Where parents and schools can welcome their children back into a kind of normal life, the outcome is more positive.

FLASHBACKS

Schlenger *et al.* (1992) found that Vietnam veterans still suffered from PTSD twenty years afterwards. This amounted then to 500,000 traumatised individuals (15.25 per cent of men and 8.5 per cent of women). Within the UK, PTSD and anger are particularly common in soldiers who undertook terms of service in the Iraq and Afghanistan wars. Of these, 40 per cent had PTSD and an additional 18 per cent had a sub-threshold PTSD; proximity to war zones and appalling sights and situations exacerbated the mental after-effects.

MORAL INJURY

There is also the painful new understanding of 'moral injury'. Of particular concern to soldiers fighting in countries alongside allies who show no compassion in warfare, is the knowledge that nobody will listen to them if they complain about how a civilian or a prisoner was treated. The Victoria National Center for PTSD provides online assistance for veterans and their families. Norman and Maguen (2020), in their online paper on moral injury in the context of war, show how extreme and unprecedented life experiences are injurious and can lead to PTSD if there is an act of moral transgression that shatters moral and ethical experience.

John
John [not his real name] was a British soldier just back from a combat zone. He came with

intrusive flashbacks alternated by a numbing
sense of derealisation and depersonalisation. The
terrible injuries and memories that haunted his
days and nights and [which] led to his inability to
maintain his family life, stemmed from witnessing
the deliberate torture and murder of an unarmed
prisoner by a senior officer who was seen as a
key ally. 'It was not just that I couldn't wipe out
the memory of what I saw, but I knew that if I
protested I would be killed and if I went to my
higher-ups they could do nothing.'

Coming back from such an experience, no wonder soldiers all over the world have difficulty reconnecting with their civilian lives and their families.

There is a new civilian form of moral injury that is happening in our Covid-era societies, where those who are sensibly protecting the health of their families are being accused of cowardice and being battle-shy. This leads to the danger of an idea that being a professional and a hero involves risking death. The mental health of ambivalent frontline workers of all kinds during a pandemic is affected by moral injury. Lack of transparent leadership exacerbates this.

RAPE IN WAR

Rape in war is almost universally and dissociatively treated as either minor collateral damage or a 'normal' trophy. Indeed, the concept of 'spoils of war' awarded to male soldiers goes back to our earliest accounts of wars. In our own time, the International Criminal Court has so far not made a single conviction over the war rape of Yazidi women. Having lifted the taboo of killing, given that war is given legitimacy by governments (unlike killing in peacetime, which is illegal), rape is often seen as irrelevant.

Rape can be a deliberate instrument of war in order to humiliate a specific group, a way of creating sexual slavery of a vanquished group or individual acts of violence. Increasingly, the victims of war are 'civilians' and, despite the appalling experience of men raped in war (Corbett, 2016), these are largely women.

In Roman times, the victor was entitled to the riches and property of the vanquished, and women were deemed to be property. Despite attempts in different historical periods to ask for clemency to civilians, this has largely been ignored. Christina Lamb (2020), the chief foreign correspondent of *The Sunday Times*, made an enormous impact with her book *Our Bodies, Their Battlefields: What war does to women*, which documents this in unbearable topical detail. Of note is the extra trauma for women whose families and community will not accept them after they have been raped or will even stigmatise and punish them. The emotional predicament of rape babies is also included here.

IMPACT OF KILLING IN WAR

While soldiers are trained to manage life and death decisions and inspiring leadership minimises violent acting out, including rape, there will always be tragic errors and re-enactments. Soldiers faced with overwhelming violence who have experienced previous trauma in their life might be triggered into repetitions. Maguen and Burkman (2014) and Maguen *et al.* (2017) have worked on special programmes to aid veterans who have experienced this. It consists of a six-session module called the 'impact of killing in war' (IOK). Not all moral injury leads to PTSD but there is an important overlap. IOK provides a moral parameter of forgiveness and compassion for the self, as well as education about the complex interplay of the biopsychosocial aspects of killing in war that might cause injury.

Readers who remember the brilliant John Cleese in the British *Monty Python* television series, might recall the skit where an army recruitment office is offering travel and education to a would-be recruit, who keeps saying 'I just want to kill people'. However, the point of the skit was the reality that most people do not want to kill someone.

Post-traumatic stress disorder (PTSD) and war experience are painfully linked. Killing people is not casual. Although it has always been known that outside of the euphoria of victory, there has been a terrible cost, the diagnosis of PTSD was not used before 1980.

SHELLSHOCK

Terms such as 'shellshock' and 'combat fatigue' took time to be used. The earlier term was 'cowardice' and, from Roman times onwards, those in states of paralysis, flight and shellshock were killed. It took until 15 August 2006 for all 306 British World War soldiers executed for desertion and cowardice to be pardoned. Consider the generational suffering of the descendants of those executed for cowardice. John Byng-Hall, a family therapist and former consultant psychiatrist at the Tavistock Clinic, spoke movingly in his understanding of myths in the family (1973) of being a descendant of the famous Admiral Byng, who was shot for saving his men by not sailing into certain death. Voltaire immortalised the situation in *Candide*. Byng was shot 'pour encourager les autres' – to encourage the others.

LITERACY

War can also bring out the greatest awareness of pain, pain relief and literacy. The army alpha test, developed by Robert Yerkes and colleagues (Atwell, 1937) to evaluate US First World War recruits, found that 30 per cent were unable to read and understand newspapers and write letters home. Although such work in the USA and the UK shone more attention on illiteracy and mild intellectual disability, it was also used for eugenics purposes. Indeed, Yerkes considered that recent immigrants from southern and eastern Europe scored lower than northern European immigrants and this enhanced his views. In the UK after the Second World War, the awareness of illiteracy during the drafting process led to action. There was more concern that people could not read military instructions in warfare (rather than they had been profoundly isolated through not being able to read during peacetime) and this led to an all-party agreement for the 1944 Education Act which was implemented in 1947. It was considered inadequate to leave school at 14. An extra year was added on. It is a paradox of war that anything positive can come from such pain. Few wars bring the moral satisfaction that the Second World War did.

AUTOIMMUNE PROBLEMS

In more recent times, the controversies about 'Gulf War syndrome' led to extra psychological symptoms being noted for Gulf War veterans. A wide range of acute and chronic symptoms were experienced by Gulf War veterans between1990 and 1991 that were not experienced by non-deployed veterans. As well as PTSD, there was chronic fatigue, muscle pain, diarrhoea, rashes and cognitive impairment. On 17 November 2008, the US Department of Veterans Affairs (VA) Research Advisory Committee on Gulf War Veterans' illnesses (RAC) made the statement that Gulf War illness was real.

In 2015, Oxford University's Department of Psychiatry, under the leadership of Professors Stark and Kringelbach, published a meta-analysis of all brain research on PTSD. This was part of a larger programme on PTSD in British war veterans run by the Scars of War Foundation, based at The Queen's College, University of Oxford. This Foundation is committed to using neuroscience to advance understanding of the effects of war and disaster. A surprising finding was that, even in the absence of symptoms, trauma may have an enduring effect on brain function.

FAMILIES OF THE ARMED SERVICES

Even when the home country is not experiencing war, military personnel can be posted to danger spots anywhere in the world. This means that the families and friends of our soldiers are left to experience the terror and loss of a war situation while living in a country that considers itself 'at peace', because the fighting is elsewhere. In other words, taking a model of structural dissociation – the ANP (apparently normal personality) – we civilians can relax in a peaceful country with little thought for the war trauma another part of the world is experiencing. Boarding schools for children of the military, while hoping to offer security and an understanding of the military background, can enhance separation and attachment problems. Abuse in residential settings carries its separate damage too.

A further cornucopia of concepts

ADVERSE CHILDHOOD EXPERIENCES

Adverse childhood experiences (ACEs) are a way of documenting traumatic events in childhood and up to the age of 18. They include all forms of abuse and neglect, as well as domestic violence, drug and alcohol addiction in parents. The actual number of adverse circumstances significantly relates to negative outcomes in adulthood. It was in 1986 that Dr Vincent Felitti tried to understand the reason for so many of his patients in San Diego dropping out of obesity weight-loss programmes. It was when he asked a patient how much she had weighed when she was first sexually active, instead of her age, and she answered with details of her abuse, that he began to realise the impact of sexual abuse on obesity. He slowly realised that obesity was a defence, a 'fix' that made the pain of memory and history easier to bear. This was replicated by colleagues but evoked major controversy and disagreement. In researching with colleagues from 1995 to 1997, 17,421 people were interviewed. Dr Robert Anda, an epidemiologist, found there was a direct link with ACEs and the onset of chronic diseases, as well as mental illness, crime and other issues. The larger the number of adverse experiences the higher the risk of social, economic, physical and psychological problems.

FURTHER BIOLOGICAL AND NEURO-BIOLOGICAL ASPECTS OF TRAUMA

As discussed earlier, in common with other animals, we share certain biological and neurobiological responses to danger. The fight–flight response (Cannon, 1915) affects breathing and heart rate, and heightens vigilance. There is extra brain activity in the release of noradrenaline for the brain itself, as well as signals transmitted for the release of adrenaline. The same bodily changes happen in later situations where escape is possible, but a trigger is present or a mild aversive stimulus (Van der Kolk and Greenberg, 1987; Ogden and Fisher, 2015; Van der Kolk 2015). An immediate response of a neurobiological kind can be reversible but, where the trauma lasts or is of sufficient intensity of frequency (Perry, 1994), the changes are not reversible.

On 20 June 2019, new generation-transmission research was presented at the Fifth European Academy of Neurology

Congress. Children of Holocaust survivors show reduced connectivity between structures of the brain involved in the processing of emotion and memory. Additionally, the parent generation, the survivors of the Holocaust, showed significant decrease in grey matter in the parts of the brain responsible for memory, emotion and behaviour.

It is not surprising to trauma-informed clinicians that those who experience such major overwhelming physical and emotional assaults should have this reflected in the brain as well. It is through the Holocaust research that we are realising how many children and adults with painful emotional loads are still bearing something that occurred several generations back. This is why good government policy of housing, justice and work safeguards the future as well as the present.

INNOCENT TRAUMA

Natural disasters, which are large and public, are shared and are historical events. They are seen and accepted as fact and most people affected by them can feel 'innocent' or 'deserving' of help, sexual abuse, on the other hand, despite affecting millions in the UK, is experienced as private, shameful and guilty.

LERNER'S JUST WORLD THEORY

In lucky, peaceful countries, people largely have a benign view of the world. Lerner's (1980) 'just world theory' underlines the sense of a fair world in which people get what they deserve. If you work hard and do good, then good things will happen to you. Trauma calls into question all these ways of viewing the self and the world (Bard and Sangrey, 1970; Janoff-Bulman, 1985; Garland, 1998). Trauma is not fair. It destroys the innocent and guilty. It activates religious, social and personal doubts, and destroys the assumptions of a fair world full of natural justice.

When lucky clinicians and clients speak of next year's events or a planned project, they often do not realise how this reveals their 'just world' belonging. Some people cannot be sure of what will happen in an hour let alone in a week. Oscar Wilde's (1895) famous aphorism, 'the good ended happily, and the bad unhappily. That is what Fiction means', used humour to expose the positive delusion that can come from a positive view of the world (*The Importance of Being Ernest*).

It was thanks to the lessons provided by people who had experienced trauma that I learned not to say 'See you next week', but instead 'I hope to see you next week'. The Islamic greeting 'See you tomorrow, inshallah' (God willing) underlines the truth that apart from mortality, the only certainty is uncertainty. A trauma-informed approach to time and communicating can make a significant difference here. 'Goodbye – I hope to see you next week.'

With coronavirus, we are all learning how to live with uncertainty.

STOCKHOLM SYNDROME

This is the term given for a condition in which a hostage develops a life-saving alliance with a captor during captivity. There was no previous relationship between them. The term came from an incident in Stockholm in 1973 when employees of a bank were held hostage for six days. A close relationship developed, which evoked surprise in the outside world. If a group of employed adults could develop such a relationship after only six days, we gain an idea of the life experience of an abused child or adult.

THE NON-INNOCENT BYSTANDER

Dr Petruska Clarkson (1947–2006) was one of the founders of the Metanoia Institute in 1984, dedicated to a humanistic and libertarian training. A South-African psychotherapist, she came to the UK in 1977. She pointed out that in most conflicts in the world, the victims and the perpetrators stood out clearly and were often the smallest number. The largest number, who had not been previously so clearly focused on, were the non-innocent bystanders. Catherine Sanderson (2020) has recently provided a further exploration of those ideas, showing, for example, the impact of 'social loafing', when we think that someone else will help in a situation where a large number of people witness something. This idea of 'social loafing' links with the research conducted by Stanley Milgram (1963) which showed that, out of obedience to authority, many people who had been asked to be involved in a learning experiment were willing to inflict what they thought was real pain. Indeed, the fake electric shock they were encouraged to inflict (on actors) would have been fatal at the most severe level, if real. As with social loafing, the non-innocent bystander can become a perpetrator when ordered to do something by someone in authority.

WINNICOTT'S THREE TRAUMAS (SINASON, 2003a)

Let us return to the inside again. And to the start of life where the first impingements begin. Babies can hear in utero the shouts of warring people around them, are affected by violence to the pregnant host, by drugs and alcohol in the mother's body.

Winnicott considered **birth trauma** could constitute significant impingements on a baby and child's development. For example, pain experienced as a band round the head, chest restriction and breathing problems could be a result of birth trauma.

Mary

Mary, aged 13, had problems with swallowing,
|drinking and eating. She upset staff by saying her
food was poisoned. It emerged from her notes that
her mother had been an alcoholic and Mary's mild
intellectual disability had links to fetal alcohol poisoning.

Winnicott also considered each failure in environmental attunement as part of the compound features that could lead to traumatic adaptation in the child. This has similarities with Masud Khan's cumulative trauma.

The third feature was the **false self** (Winnicott, 1960) as a traumatic development. When the parent is not able to adapt to being 'good enough', the infant is forced into a false compliant mode of being, hiding its true self to protect it from 'the unthinkable, the exploitation of the True Self, which would result in its annihilation' (p.147). Orbach (2002) has taken this into the realm of the physical body with her delineation of the false body.

BOARDING SCHOOL SYNDROME

In my book *Mental Handicap and the Human Condition,* published in 1992, I wrote what I had observed and commented on in countless lectures: '...every year upper-class children face their own culturally accepted act of abandonment in being sent away from home and having to smile about it.' Most child therapists are middle class or have become middle class through their training. There is a profound class difference between upper-class or aristocratic children and middle-class ones that is rarely discussed. In his 1973 work *Separation: Anxiety and anger*, John Bowlby wrote on how bad boarding school was for him. 'I wouldn't send a dog away to boarding school at age seven.' He did, however, note the situations in which boarding school could be helpful. For example, where a parent was ill and could not manage, or where stability was needed when a parent or parents had to frequently move. In the last two decades, Joy Schaverien (2015) and Nick Duffell (2000) have been the British psychotherapists who have written most about this. Having to be pseudo-self-reliant at a young age, deal with separation and loss with a fake smile, and learn that your feelings will not be contained and understood is a wound in the psyche of many upper-class and aristocratic children.

POST-TRAUMATIC SLAVERY SYNDROME

In the 1980s, a young teenage black man was more or less sentenced to psychotherapy. Brought in by two burly charge nurses, he loudly swore: 'I don't want no fucking whitey to talk to.' The two men moved to restrain him and I asked them to leave. 'Why would you want to talk to a fucking whitey after what whiteys have done to you and your family?' He looked slightly surprised and I pointed to the armchair opposite me. I said, 'The problem is, how do we help you stand up for your history and your people without you getting put in chains in a different way?' Like many therapists, I was aware of the generational transmission of slavery, as powerful as Holocaust generational transmission. However, it is only in the last two decades that the significance of this as a diagnosis has been recognised. Joy DeGruy (2005) drew this to American attention in her seminal book. It is such a relatively short time ago that slavery flourished. It clearly still does but in a more illegal, hidden way. The emotional impact of centuries of oppression and, in America, lynchings, the Jim Crow laws and so forth, require social change to aid recovery. The murder of George Floyd in May 2020 in Minneapolis has highlighted institutional racism in police all over the world.

FREUD'S REPETITION COMPULSION

Among many of his brilliant theories, Freud's (1914) concept of repetition compulsion is particularly helpful in terms of understanding trauma. He realised that where something was not amenable to memory because of its traumatic content, it would be acted out again and again without the patient realising. One of the difficult consequences of this is that by repeating behaviours blindly instead of remembering, the individual can put themselves into the very situation where a repeat could happen. George Santayana, the Spanish American philosopher(1863–1952), put this in clear terms for all (1905): 'Those who cannot remember the past are condemned to repeat it.'

Mary had been raped in a piece of woodland at 13 and, to her family's relief, forgot about it. However, at 16 she kept walking alone to the same area and was assaulted there.

JENNIFER FREYD'S INSTITUTIONAL BETRAYAL AND CULTURAL BETRAYAL

Jennifer Freyd, an outstanding researcher and psychology professor, understands these subjects from a double perspective. It is sadly her lived experience; her parents were the founders of the American False Memory Society, which has just dissolved, and tried to publicly silence and discredit their adult daughter. The usefulness of her concept of betrayal trauma is that it is often forgotten that a child has been betrayed in the very place they should have been supported and validated.

Betrayal trauma The phrase 'betrayal trauma' can be used to refer to a kind of trauma independent of the reaction to the trauma (Freyd, 2008). *Betrayal trauma occurs when the people or institutions on which a person depends for survival significantly violate that person's trust or well-being: Childhood physical, emotional, or sexual abuse perpetrated by a caregiver are examples of betrayal trauma.*

Betrayal trauma theory From Sivers *et al.* (2002): *A theory that predicts that the degree to which a negative event represents a betrayal by a trusted needed other will influence the way in which that event is processed and remembered.*

Betrayal blindness and institutional betrayal Betrayal blindness is the unawareness, not-knowing and forgetting exhibited by people towards betrayal. The term 'betrayal blindness' was introduced by Freyd, and expanded in Freyd (1999) and Freyd and Birrell (2013) in the context of betrayal trauma theory. This blindness may extend to betrayals that are not traditionally considered 'traumas', such as adultery, inequities in the workplace and society, etc. Victims, perpetrators and witnesses may display betrayal blindness in order to preserve relationships, institutions and social systems upon which they depend.

The concept 'institutional betrayal' refers to wrong-doings perpetrated by an institution upon individuals dependent on that institution, including failure to prevent or respond supportively to wrong-doings by individuals (e.g. sexual assault) committed within the context of the institution.

The term 'cultural betrayal' covers both internalising the racism from outside, but also dealing with estrangement from inside when your own group lets you down.

FALSE MEMORY SYNDROME

This is not a proper syndrome. However, societal fear at addressing the extensive reality of childhood abuse has provided a remarkable level of media exposure for those espousing this term. This has made even well-trained professionals consider that it is worryingly extensive. Forensic professionals working with burglars, for example, do not have to be acquainted with 'false burglar recognition syndrome'. Professionals working with those who wet their beds do not have to check the sheets. Nor do patients who speak of nightmares and difficulties sleeping have to go through a lie detector test before they are helped. Only in the field of child abuse and organised abuse do professionals have to contend with not just the pain of the subject and the unbearableness of the reality some children and adults exist in, but also the slandering from allegedly innocent adults.

Professionals in the field of trauma are aware that memory is open to distortion. There are a small number of patients who name the wrong person. This is traumatic and abusive for any innocent victim. There are also, across all crimes, a small number of people who are wrongly convicted. However, the public relations success of this term around the world is of concern for the damage it has caused to those who are silenced and denigrated by it.

The American False Memory Syndrome Foundation was founded in 1992 and dissolved on 31 December 2019. It was created by Professor Jennifer Freyd's parents who, like several of the parents who joined such associations, created public arenas for what their adult children only said privately to them. Ralph Underwager, an early member, resigned from the Board after he was found to have written in *Paedika: The Journal of Paedophilia*. The British False Memory Society was founded by Roger Scotford in 1993 after one of his adult daughters privately alleged abuse. He made her private accusation public. He told me he felt a ray of hope when he heard about the American organisation and decided to create a British one. He regularly attended my lectures on memory and abuse and was always personally polite and interested. He died in 2018.

One mother, Mary, who turned out to be wrongly accused by her adult daughter, came for therapy to understand what could have caused such confusion in her daughter.

I love my daughter and I was not going to publicly shame her or join an organisation for the innocent and the allegedly innocent. If some of my daughter's confused state came unwittingly from me, I needed to take responsibility.

She was able to realise in therapy that her own childhood abuse, which she had been silent about, had somehow impacted on her daughter's sense of sexual safety.

We were able to understand together that some of the ways I physically was with her carried my own past trauma and she was aware something wasn't comfortable, and in her late teens and early 20s, she thought I must have abused her.

Unworked-through trauma gets passed on generationally. Mary did not publish her daughter's name or denounce the therapeutic and psychiatric treatment she had received. She took responsibility for whatever part she might have unwittingly played, and mother and daughter now have a solid relationship.

The hard therapeutic work that allows such understanding takes emotional responsibility. Unfortunately, the terror of being publicly attacked, complained about and discredited can affect professionals and survivors alike. Indeed, the inclusion of third-party complaints can sometimes make professional bodies forget who the patient is. Trauma-informed workers are only too aware of litigious adults trying to pursue their grown-up children, who have capacity, by complaining to commissioning bodies and ethics bodies.

CONTROLLING OR COERCIVE BEHAVIOUR

Controlling or coercive behaviour in an intimate or family relationship was finally accepted as a crime in the December 2015 Statutory Guidance Framework.

The Serious Crime Act 2015 (the 2015 Act) received Royal Assent on 3 March 2015. The Act creates a new offence of controlling or coercive behaviour in intimate or familial relationships (section 76). The new offence closes a gap in the law around patterns of controlling or coercive behaviour in an ongoing relationship between intimate partners or family members. The offence carries a maximum sentence of five years' imprisonment, a fine or both.

The law defines coercive control as a 'continuing act, or pattern of acts, of assault, threats, humiliation and intimidation or other abuse that is used to harm, punish, or frighten their victim'.

GASLIGHTING

One of the tactics of the Stasi, the German secret police, was to manipulate a victim's mind by entering their home and just slightly moving familiar objects an inch or so. This subtle sense of disorientation, with there being no proof of house breaking, can be understood in the use of the new term 'gaslighting'. Gaslighting, as a manipulative tactic in which a person makes a victim question their reality, gains its name from a popular play in 1938, *Gas Light*. It later became a film in 1944, with Ingrid Bergman in the female role. In this story a man, Gregory, manipulates his wife to the point where she thinks she is losing her sanity. The term 'gaslight' in the play and film comes from Gregory convincing his wife that her sense of lights going on and off was due to her own disturbance. In fact, he was switching the attic lights on and off.

WE ARE GETTING BETTER EVERY DAY AND THE MYTHICAL RESPONSE TO TRAUMA

Each person is the professor of their own trauma and needs to find the books, activities and people that aid their path. For some, there is indeed help to be gained from bright and breezy books full of aspirational text. For some, words like 'recovery', 'healing' and 'enrichment' really do work.

However, spare a thought for all the exceptions: those whose suffering does not make them noble and wiser. Suffering adds to the burdens a human carries. Pain shortens our emotional fuses. There are those who can never trust another human being and spend their emotional energy destroying any relationship they could have out of fear.

- Small children, already excluded from every exclusion unit.
- Homeless adults.
- Those on the back wards of failing
- institutions, or the backstreets.
- Those who drink spirits to make up for the spirit they have lost.

- Those who attack every helping friend or professional they meet while continuing to idealise abusing family members.
- Those who abuse and kill themselves and their family or others.

Spare a thought for those who cannot leave the internal or external trauma they live within, because it is their known world and only safety.

Dr John Lazarus of Newcastle University answered this for me when he wondered why antelope grazed in front of their main predator, the lions on African plains. The answer was so simple. The only moment of safety to graze was when you could see your predator, the lion, had already eaten and was sleepy. If you left, you might bump into a herd of ravenous lions. Please pass this research on. It is so obvious and shame-reducing. Think of the child or adult whose safe moment is when the drunken abuser is asleep. Why risk going elsewhere?

Spare a thought for those who are told that leaving abusive families will lead to immediate emotional liberation and then find the pain of feeling orphaned worse than anything they ever experienced during the abuse. For those who had not realised how their family identity was so inextricably woven into their veins, that trying to extract family leaves scarred emptiness. For those condemned for not hating their familial abusers but loving them.

Spare a thought for those from minority groups who fear stigmatisation and more racism if abuse is disclosed, and so try to silence their members. For those from minorities who find themselves in a minority of one when they leave. To be the minority of a minority is a further trauma. Those who have a cultural social identity can lose more than they ever realised when they leave, if there is no welcome elsewhere.

Spare a thought for age and the way that each year over a legal age of majority that someone stays enslaved, the more they punish themselves for not leaving. Think too of those who leave early and feel unable to say how abandoned and unloved they feel when others only want to say they are brave for leaving.

Spare a thought for those whose involuntary sexual response to violence, as a bodily way of survival, is used to shame them.

Spare a thought for shame: for some it is one of the basic, irreducible, pre-verbal feelings, together with disgust, fear, joy, surprise. For others, it is a secondary emotion. It is the most corrosive – the squirming unbearableness of the discrepancy between self-regard and another's cruel and shaming impingement.

Spare a thought for the possible pain under the smart appearance, bright smile and magnificent home as much as the pain under dishevelled and unwashed loss.

Spare a thought for those made ill by problems with 'benefits' (Mind, 2017), austerity and living in poverty.

Spare a thought for those in the aristocracy and upper class suffering from boarding school syndrome and being the second son or the unwanted daughter.

For all those we cannot help but who still need containment of a humane kind.

And spare a thought for yourself, dear Reader.

An ending that cannot conclude

The whistle-stop tour is over. A whistle-stop tour accompanied, hopefully by whistle-blowers! The word 'whistle-blower' dates to the nineteenth century, where a whistle was used to alert the general public or a crowd about something wrong or dangerous happening at that moment. Whistles were also, of course, used by referees in sports. A whistle was and is also carried by police officers, to be heard above the sound of the traffic. It now means someone who informs on or exposes wrongs in the world. The National Health Service has put in protective procedures around this action to ensure that an employee is not sacked for reporting on corruption or unethical behaviour in public service. The whistle-blower threatens either the status quo or a silenced subject. In a way, the whistle-blower on trauma is like the messenger. 'Don't shoot the messenger' is a reminder of an unwritten code for warfare made in earliest times. The messenger bringing bad news is frightened of being hated but puts their responsibility for providing the message first.

Those who speak of childhood trauma, or war atrocities, of trafficked women and children, of the involvement of all social classes in organised abuse, are not popular.

On 25 June 1942, the *Daily Telegraph* published a remarkable story with the headline 'Germans murder 700,000 Jews in Poland'. The facts for the article were smuggled into England by Szmul Zygielbojm, from the Polish government-in-exile. It also mentioned gas chambers and the murder of children in orphanages and the sick in hospitals. It was published on the fifth page of the paper and was not picked up. The author, whose family died in the Warsaw Ghetto, committed suicide a year later. He stands for all those who risked their lives bringing the bad news that could not be tolerated.

Famous BBC journalist and broadcaster, the late Sir Richard Dimbleby, was the first reporter to enter the Belsen concentration camp in April 1945. The BBC initially refused to play the report as they could not believe the scenes he had described. It was broadcast after he threatened to resign if they did not. This not only shows his integrity but also his power as a brilliant broadcaster. They did not want to lose him. History is filled with the torn papers, manuscripts, the unexamined archaeology of truth.

On 27 January 2019, on Holocaust Day, 45 per cent of those polled did not know how many had been killed and 19 per cent thought under two million Jews were murdered;

5 per cent did not believe the Holocaust existed (www.hmd. org.uk/news/we-release-research-to-mark-holocaust-memorial-day-2019).

Having read this short book, such facts are probably less likely to surprise you. The unbearableness of reality inevitably destroys thinking capacity at times.

The myth of Cassandra is very helpful here (Sinason and Conway, 2020). Cassandra was the Greek prophetess who was given the gift of prophecy and could see and report every danger coming. Of course, she was never believed. How did it happen that she bore this terrible curse and gift? Tragically, it emerges she refused the sexual pressure of Apollo who punished her in this way. Sexual abuse was behind silencing and stating the truth as far back as we can go.

Only 30 years ago child abuse was thought to be a minor problem only involving a few hundred children. Adult psychotherapy departments could even proudly say 'We have never seen any abused adult here'. Practitioners who spoke of hearing about such trauma from their patients were seen as having disturbed minds. This means anyone now over 40 who tried to tell an adult or a professional about abuse was unlikely to be heard properly. The same applied to professionals. I was interviewed by a psychiatrist after stating that a child with an intellectual disability could have been abused. It was not considered possible that the rapist would have such bad taste! This was, after all, the time in which a woman was blamed for attracting the attention of a rapist by her dress.

Although professionals in the field of intellectual disability were quicker than others to realise that our client group could have gone through all the worst that is possible, the response to adults, especially young adult women, talking about incest, was punitive. The American False Memory Society has now dissolved (2020) but its damaging legacy lingers on. Even at a time when the British False Memory Society only consisted of a couple of hundred parents of adult women, the media, to their shame, were largely more interested in photographs of grieving, allegedly innocent parents than in the slow understanding of the sexual trauma and memory that had built up in their adult children. Complaints made by parents about their adult children's therapy were listened to by frightened commissioning groups, which lost sight of who the patient was. Fear is as contagious as a virus. Indeed, the Department of Health now considers that 11 million adults in the UK are likely to have experienced abuse. This far outweighs coronavirus in its numbers and destructive powers, but shame and silencing lessen the shock of such figures.

Of course, out of 11 million people, a very small percentage of people have been known to give misleading or wrong evidence and it is an abuse to be wrongly accused. However, government, professional and survivor organisations have major concerns for the huge percentage of victims whose cases are not taken up or who lack the strength to report because of the cutbacks in legal aid and the silencing and criticism of major police enquiries.

Few of us can stand up consistently to the moral courage needed to whistle-blow against these attitudes. It is how to be ethical-enough.

Uncovering the reasons for a patient or a friend or a family member's ill-health does not bring a bouquet and a pay rise. It can bring a painful paradigm shift and slanderous attacks on social media. Our professional bodies used to look after us but now claim to be protecting 'the public' – which all too often means allegedly innocent attackers. Our insurance for slander does not cover areas like this and, when we are acquitted from such attacks, it is not public in the way a court case would be. We therefore need to look after ourselves.

When I first encountered a narrative of ritual abuse (Sinason, 1994) from an intellectually disabled woman in Sweden, it made me feel ill and I could not speak about it for months. When I finally did mention it, in the last line of a speech in Scotland about child abuse, I was besieged with calls to the Tavistock Clinic from white, middle-class, professional women telling me about their histories. I have never felt as ill in my life. These were details of torture. I became aware of an invisible abuse. But when I researched it and shared it with others, my second most low period followed. This was due to the lack of immediate or appropriate action from the police, Parliament and the helping professions. It also led to the experience of being professionally slandered by 'false memory' devotees. As a third-generation Londoner, grateful to a liberal democracy, I could now see through my own lived experience the power of disinformation, lack of adequate ethical investigative reporting, lack of adequate policing and the pressure to be silent. Slowly, the courage of survivors and survivor organisations and the strength of friends and professionals and good police officers created extra containment for the work. If I could feel like this as a lucky professional, what was it like for a survivor, who not only had an unbearable narrative but relied on non-equipped and untrained professionals to help them?

Truth, however, is always revealed in the end. For those of us in this field there is a moral imperative. This is no 9-to-5 work. And we are privileged to meet some of the finest human beings we could ever meet. And this includes you, dear Reader, in daring to read what you did not want to know. For who does want to hear of such horrors? After my first disappointment in clinicians who did not want to take up this work, I later realised they were being sensible in terms of their own emotional resources. Who would want this work if it did not come to them and land on them?

One morning I decided I would respond to each beggar in the street where I live. Instead of making them invisible and walking on, I would either give them something or say 'sorry' and look them in the eye. I managed this for three people and then gave up. I walked past the fourth who loudly shouted, 'Thank you for not noticing me and a good day to you too.' I could not expand to include this person. The secret inside trauma is that we all need to become dissociative at times.

So how are you, Reader? Time to open a window and look out at the world? To listen to music? To dance? Water the plants? How do you resource yourself? Trauma impacts on us, mind, body and soul. There is no one therapy or action that answers everything. I first trained in child psychotherapy at the Tavistock Clinic (where I later became a consultant), which was psychoanalytically orientated, and then at the Institute of Psychoanalysis for an adult training. Psychoanalysis as a body of theory and an application has been a major resource for me personally and professionally, combined with my own psychoanalysis. However, in working with extreme trauma it has been clear that all kinds of resources are needed. The creative therapies, energy therapies, body therapies, psychodynamic, humanist, relational, attachment and cognitive therapies are all important. Sometimes, walking while speaking about trauma can act as EMDR (eye movement desensitisation and deprocessing), sometimes composing music, singing, painting, dancing, baking, gardening, looking after children, planning a career can also help. For those who have religious beliefs, and for those who do not practise a religion but have a sense of the spiritual, there are also spiritual resources.

As well as the brilliant survivor professionals who have become known to us, there are many more out there who do not speak publicly about their own position. 'Until the stigma has gone it would ruin my career to say I have DID and am a psychiatrist', said June, who gave me permission to mention her. 'My DID is stable so I can trust the children [inside child personalities] to stay away for the three days a week I work and earn money for us all'. The different levels of trauma that live in all of us varies and, with DID, as with other signs of trauma, it matters whether it is stable (Sachs, 2017) or volatile in order to conduct professional work. Anna Freud, in her notes for teachers, spoke of a governess who did brilliantly with a girl who was the family 'ugly duckling'. She poured love into her and the child blossomed. But once the child blossomed, the governess no longer cared for her. Anna Freud used that example to show why professionals working with the vulnerable needed to look at themselves carefully (1930).

Physician heal thyself. It needs repeating again and again. We are all walking the history of our species and if we are privileged with hearing the private discourse of another, we owe it to them to know ourselves as well as we can.

Which aspects of trauma can we manage? Why? Which aspects of trauma are too unbearable for us? Why? Before starting with any new patient, ask yourself: 'What trauma am I most fearful of coming close to?' That will inform you of family areas that are not resolved.

At one level everything in this book is familiar. And every trauma is familiar. It is what you have always known, even if you did not want to know it. We are a flawed species who find our sexuality and aggression hard to deal with, as well as our fear of rejection, loss and our mortality. As such:

- **There is a trauma.**
  It includes a suddenness of attack that cannot be prepared for, that is intentional or perceived as such; the proximity and severity of the attack matter and it must be outside normal experience and involve a fear of dying.

- **When it happens, it obviously leads to internal consequences as our psyches have to react.**
  The impact includes biological and neurobiological change, terror, shame, loss of love or perceived loss, annihilation anxiety and fear, unconscious guilt, breakdown of a sense of a just world, helplessness and hypervigilance.

- **These processes are ameliorated or exacerbated by:**
  Nature of attachment, age, previous history of trauma, protective features in the environment and resilience in the self.
- **Further danger after the trauma**
  This includes re-traumatisation, which can occur at the moment there is cognitive awareness of the trauma, past or present; a loving relationship can activate terror of unbearable loss. There can be sexualising of fear, terror, excessive control or risk-taking; all the defences needed to survive: delinquency or violent re-enactment, mental illness, phobias, somatisation, addiction. Each new stage of life reawakens old triggers, right through to old age.

It is so simple and yet so impossible.

Becoming trauma-informed is the chance of making a real difference to society, and of reducing the proliferation of specialisms. Indeed, we could perhaps think that trauma and dissociation induce a defence of splitting into dissociative fragments in all services, adult and child, psychiatric, forensic, depressive, somatic, addiction (mad, bad, sad, sick, suck). We ask our patients to dare to listen to all the wisdom inside 'their-selves'. Can we do that for ourselves?

There will be people we cannot help. There will be all kinds of problems. However, staying truthful, relational and authentic will aid the path. Even one such patient enriches the rest of our understanding and life, as they will know our weaknesses better than most of our therapists. Their lives have depended on reading faces and bodies and accommodating dangerous adults.

So, when we encounter another human being in our personal life, our professional life, our research, our reading, we can consider that they are carrying, lightly or heavily, their own unique history and that we are carrying ours. A gift that came from psychoanalysis was the neutrality of not being judgemental, echoed by the saying 'Before you judge a man, walk a mile in his moccasins'. Our language, our relating, our respect for one another, our nurturing of dignity – it is only us. And us. Meanwhile, a virus moves around the human known world. It will return again and again. It does not need a passport or respond to one. It ignores walls and Brexits. But love and attachment also circle the globe without frontiers. They are illimitable universes. We are always, as a species, struggling with love in the shadow of death, but sometimes it is more visible. Adam Phillips (1995) aptly commented 'Firstly, you can only tell yourself a secret by telling someone else. And secondly, people are only ever as mad (unintelligible) as other people are deaf (unable or unwilling to listen).

It is not only beauty that is the beginning of terror, it's also listening.'

Thank you for hearing the voices that have come through me for whatever extent you have. We cannot deny the terror. It has always been there. But so has the beauty.

Isn't it remarkable to consider that as a living being, we are part of a history of humankind with ancestors in all previous periods? It has taken us nearly three-quarters of a century to bear the links to the Second World War which all our ancestors and families went through. Some traumas take generations to pass through and be slowly smoothed into a polished stone of memory. Only now, in this my eighth decade have I made the links to the missing generations before my parents and realised more deeply the reasons for my involvement in this subject. We are living in historical times and how we negotiate trauma, the visible and the unseen will affect the new world we make. To life!

> We shall not cease from exploration, and the end
> of all our exploring will be to arrive where we
> started and know the place for the first time.

T.S. Eliot, *The Four Quartets* (1943)

An ending that cannot conclude

And does this poem read differently now?

And when we speak we are afraid
Our words will not be heard
Nor welcomed
But when we are silent
We are still afraid
So it is better to speak
Remembering
We were never meant to survive

Audre Lorde, *The Black Unicorn: Poems*, 1995

REFERENCES

Ainsworth, M.D. (1964), 'Patterns of attachment behaviour shown by the infant in interaction with his mother', *Merrill–Palmer Quarterly of Behavior and Development*, 51–8.

Ainsworth, M.D. and Bell, S.M. (1970), 'Attachment, exploration, and separation: illustrated by the behaviour of one year olds in a strange situation'. *Child Development*, 41, 49–67.

Ainsworth, M.D. and Wittig, B.A. (1969), 'Attachment and exploratory behaviour of one year olds in a strange situation', in Foss, B. M. (ed.), *Determinants of Infant Behaviour*, vol. 4, pp. 111–36, London: Methuen.

American Psychiatric Association (2013), *Diagnostic and Statistical Manual of Mental Disorders* (5th edn.), Washington, DC: APA.

Amnesty International (2019), *South Korea: Serving in Silence: LGBT people in South Korea's Military*, 11 July, London: Amnesty International.

Atwell, C.R. (1937), 'Relationships of scores and errors on the army alpha test', *Journal of Applied Psychology*, 21(4), 451.

Aurelius, Marcus (1964), *Meditations*, trans. Maxwell Staniforth, Book Seven. New York: Penguin Classics.

Badouk Epstein, O., Schwartz, J. and Wingfield Schwartz, R. (2011), *Ritual Abuse and Mind Control: The manipulation of attachment needs*, London: Routledge.

Baez, Joan (1997), 'February Lyrics'. Accessed March 2020: www.lyrics.com/lyric/5261289/Joan+Baez.

Bard, M. and Sangrey, D. (1970), *The Crime Victim's Book*, New York: Basic Books.

Bowlby, J. (1950). *Maternal Care and Mental Health* (The Master Works Series) (2nd edn.). Reprinted in 1995 by Jason Aronson Inc., Northvale, NJ.

Bowlby, J. (1953), *Child Care and the Growth of Love*, London: Penguin Books.

Bowlby, J. (1969, 1982), *Attachment and Loss*, vol. 1: *Attachment* (2nd edn.), New York: Basic Books.

Bowlby, J. (1973), *Attachment and Loss*, vol. 2: *Separation: Anxiety and Anger*, London: Hogarth Press.

References

Bowlby, J. (1979a), 'On knowing what you are not supposed to know and feeling what you are not supposed to feel', *Canadian Journal of Psychiatry*, 24(5), 403–8.

Bowlby, J. (1979b), *The Making and Breaking of Affectional Bonds*, London: Tavistock Publications.

Bowlby, J. (1980), *Attachment and Loss*, vol. 3, *Loss, Sadness and Depression*, London: Hogarth Press.

Brand, B.L. and Brown, Daniel J. (2016), 'An update on research about the validity, assessment, and treatment of DID', *The Dissociative Mind in Psychoanalysis*, Howell, E. F. and Itzkowitz, S. (eds), London and New York: Relational Perspective Books/Routledge.

Brewin, C. R. (2019), 'Complex post-traumatic stress disorder: a new diagnosis in IDC-11', *BJPsych Advances*, 26(3).

Byng-Hall, J. (1973), 'Family myths used as defence in conjoint family therapy', *British Journal of Medical Psychology*, 46(3), 239–50.

Cannon, W.B. (1915), *Bodily Changes in Pain, Hunger, Fear and Rage*, New York: D. Appleton & Co.

Cannon, W. (1932), *Wisdom of the Body*, New York: Norton.

Carroll, L. (1872), 'The Walrus and the Carpenter' in *Through the Looking Glass*, London: Macmillan.

Clarkson, P. (1995), *The Therapeutic Relationship*, London: Whurr Publishers.

Clarkson, P. (1996), *The Bystander: An end to innocence in human relationships*, London: Whurr Publishers.

Confucius. *The Analects* (trans. D. C. Lau, 1979 edn), London: Penguin.

Corbett, A. (2016), *Psychotherapy with Male Survivors of Sexual Abuse: The invisible men*, London: Routledge.

Daily Mirror (2019), News report, 22nd June.

Daphna-Tekoah, S. and Harel-Shalev, A. (2017), 'The Politics of Trauma Studies: An analysis of women combatants' experience of traumatic events in conflict zones', *Political Psychology*, 38(6), 943–57.

Defoe, D. (1711), 'A Review, vol. 8, entry for Saturday 15 September'. Quoted in Boulton, J.T. (ed.) (1965) *Daniel Defoe*, pp. 130–1, London: Batsford.

DeGruy, J. (2005), *Post-Traumatic Slave Syndrome: America's legacy of enduring injury and healing*, Milwaukie, OR: Uptone Press.

Department of Defense (2019) *Fiscal Year 2018 Annual Report on Sexual Assault in the Military*, Washington, USA.

References

Duffell, N. (2000), *The Making of Them: The British attitude to children and the boarding school system*, London: Lone Arrow Press.

Eliot, T.S. (1943), *Four Quartets*, New York: Harcourt, Brace and Company.

https://endcorporalpunishment.org/. Global initiative to end all corporal punishment of children.

Fairbairn, R. (1952, 1981 (reprint)), *Psychoanalytic Studies of the Personality*, London: Routledge & Kegan Paul.

Felitti, V.J., Anda, R.F., Nordenberg, D., Edwards, V., Koss, M.P. and Marks, J.S. (1998) 'Relationship of Childhood Abuse and Household Dysfunction to Many of the Leading Causes of Death in Adults. The Adverse Childhood Experiences (ACE) Study', *American Journal of Preventive Medicine*, 14(4), 245–58.

Ferenczi, S. (1929), 'The Unwelcome Child and His Death-Instinct', *The International Journal of Psychoanalysis*, 10, 125–9.

Figley, C. (ed.) (2002), *Treating Compassion Fatigue*, Psychosocial Stress Series, New York: Brunner-Routledge.

Fisher, L. (2019), 'Army "systemically racist" black soldiers tell tribunal', *The Times*, 3 July.

Fonagy, P. (2006), 'The mentalisation-focused approach to social development' in Allen, J. and Fonagy, P. (eds), *Handbook of Mentalisation Based Treatments*, London: Wiley.

Fonagy, P. and Target, M. (1995), 'Dissociation and trauma', *Current Opinion in Psychiatry*, 8, 161–6.

Frank, Anne (1947; 1993 (reprint)), *The Diary of a Young Girl*, New York: Bantam.

Freud, A. (1930), 'Four Lectures on Psychoanalysis for Teachers and Parents', *The Writings of Anna Freud, Volume 1 1922–1935*, pp. 73–136, New York: International Universities Press.

Freud, S. (1893), 'On the psychical mechanism of hysterical phenomena', Standard Edition 3, 27–39.

Freud, S. (1914), 'Remembering, Repeating and Working-Through (Further Recommendations on the Technique of Psychoanalysis II)', Standard Edition 12, 145–56.

Freud, S. (1926), 'Inhibitions, symptoms and anxiety', Standard Edition 20.

Freyd, J.J. (1997), 'Violations of power, adaptive blindness, and betrayal

References

trauma theory', *Feminism & Psychology*, 7(1), 22–32.

Freyd, J.J. (1998), *Betrayal Trauma: The logic of forgetting childhood abuse*, Cambridge, MA.: Harvard University Press.

Freyd, J.J. (1999), 'Blind to betrayal: New perspectives on memory for trauma', *The Harvard Medical Health Letters*, 15(12), 4–6.

Freyd, J.J. (2008), 'Betrayal trauma', in Reyes *et al.* (eds), *The Encyclopaedia of Psychological Trauma*, New York: Wiley. https://dynamic.uoregon.edu/jjf/articles/freyd2008bt.pdf.

Freyd, J.J. and Birrell, P.J. (2013), *Blind to Betrayal*, New York: Wiley.

Garland, C. (1991), 'External disasters and the internal world: An approach to psychotherapeutic understanding of survivors' in Holmes, J. (ed.), *Textbook of Psychotherapy in Psychiatric Practice*, London: Churchill Livingstone.

Garland, C. (1998), 'What is a trauma?' in Garland, C. (ed.) *Understanding Trauma: A psychoanalytical approach*, pp. 9–31, London: Duckworth.

Harel-Shalev, A. and Daphna-Tekoah, S. (2016), 'The "Double Battle": Women combatants and embodied experiences in warzones', *Critical Studies on Terrorism*, 9(2), 312–33.

Harel-Shalev, A. and Daphna-Tekoah, S. (2020), *Breaking the Binaries in Trauma Studies: A gendered analysis of women in combat*, Oxford: OUP.

Harlow, H.F., Dodsworth, R.O. and Harlow, M.K. (1965), 'Total social isolation in monkeys', *Proceedings of the National Academy of Sciences of the United States of America*, 54(1), 90–7.

Harrington, C. (2011), 'Resolution 1325 and Post-Cold War Feminist Politics', in *International Feminist Journal of Politics*, 13(4), 557–75.

Hart, O., Nijenhuis, E.R.S. and Steele, K. (2006), *The Haunted Self: Structural dissociation and the treatment of chronic traumatization*, New York: Norton.

Hartman, C. and Burgess, A. (1985), 'Illness-related post-traumatic disorder' in Figley, C. (ed.), *Trauma and its Wake*, New York: Brunner/Mazel.

Hesse, E. and Main, M. (1999), 'Second Generation Effects of Unresolved Trauma in Non-Maltreating Parents: Dissociated, frightened and threatening parental behaviour', *Psychoanalytic Inquiry*, 19(4), 481–540.

Hollins, S. and Sinason, V. (2000), 'Psychotherapy, Learning Disabilities and Trauma: New perspectives', *British Journal of Psychiatry*, 176(1), 32–6.

References

Hopkins, G.M. (1885), Poem: 'I wake and feel the fell of dark, not day'. Later published in *Gerard Manley Hopkins: Poems and Prose* (pub. 1985), London: Penguin.

Howell, E. (2020), *Trauma and Dissociation-Informed Psychotherapy: Relational healing and the therapeutic connection*, New York: Norton.

Jamieson, A. (2009), *Today I'm Alice: Nine personalities, one tortured mind*, London: Pan Macmillan.

Janoff-Bulman, R. (1985), 'The Aftermath of Victimization: Rebuilding shattered assumptions' in Figley, C. (ed.), *Trauma and Its Wake: The study and treatment of post-traumatic stress disorder*, pp. 15–35. New York: Brunner/Mazel.

Kahr, B. (1993), 'Ancient Infanticide and Modern Schizophrenia: The clinical uses of psychohistory research', *Journal of Psychohistory*, 267–73.

Kahr, B. (2007), 'The Infanticidal Attachment' in *Attachment: New Directions in Psychotherapy and Relational Psychoanalysis*, 1(2), 117–232, London: Karnac Books.

Khan, M. (1963), 'The Concept of Cumulative Trauma', in *The Psychoanalytic Study of the Child*, 18(1), 286–306.

Kubler-Ross, E. (1969), *On Death and Dying*, London: Routledge.

Lamb, C. (2020), *Our Bodies, Their Battlefield: What war does to women*, London: Collins.

Lapin, T. (2017), 'LGBT soldiers are going after ISIS in Syria', *New York Post*, 25 July.

Larkin, W. and Read, J. (2008), 'Childhood Trauma and Psychosis: Evidence, pathways and implications', *Journal of Postgraduate Medicine*, 54(4), 287–93.

Lerner, M.J.K. (1980), *The Belief in a Just World*, New York: Plenum Press.

Levi, P. (1987) (first published in Italy 1958), *If This is a Man: The truce*, London: Abacus Books.

Liotti, G. (1992), 'Disorganised/disorientated attachment in the etiology of the dissociative disorders', *Dissociation*, 5, 196–204.

McCartney, P. (1982), 'Wanderlust' from the album *Tug of War*.

McQueen, D., Itzin, C., Kennedy, R., Sinason, V. and Maxted, F. (2008), *Psychoanalytic Psychotherapy After Child Abuse: The treatment of adults and children who have experienced sexual abuse, violence, and neglect in childhood*, London: Karnac Books.

Maguen, S. and Burkman, K. (2014), 'Killing in War and Moral Injury: Research and clinical considerations', 22 May. Invited lecture at the 17th Annual VA Psychology Leadership Conference, San Antonio.

Maguen, S., Burkman, K., Madden, E., Dinh, J., Bosch, J., Keyser, J., Schmitz, M. and Neylan, T.C. (2017), 'Impact of Killing in War: A randomized, controlled pilot trial', *Journal of Clinical Psychology*, 73(9).

Main, M. (1977), 'Analysis of a peculiar form of reunion behaviour seen in some day-care children', in Webb, R. (ed.), *Social Development in Childhood*, pp. 33–78. Baltimore, MD: Johns Hopkins University Press.

Main, M. (1979), 'The "Ultimate" Causation of Some Infant Attachment Phenomena', *Behavioural and Brain Sciences*, 2, 640–3.

Main, M. and Solomon, J. (1990), 'Procedures for Identifying Infants as Disorganised/Disorientated During the Ainsworth Strange Situation.' in Greenberg *et al. Attachment in the Preschool Years; Theory, research and intervention*, pp. 121–60, Chicago, IL: University of Chicago Press.

Marlowe, C. (1589), *The Jew of Malta*, Act IV, Scene 1.

Maresca, T. (2019), Amnesty International: LGBT soldiers face abuse in South Korea military, World News, *UPI*, 11 July.

Milgram, S. (1963), 'Behavioural Study of Obedience', *Journal of Abnormal and Social Psychology*, 67(4), 371–8.

Mind (2017), 'People with mental health problems made more unwell by benefits system', 17 May. Retrieved from www.mind.org.uk/news-campaigns/news/people-with-mental-health-problems-made-more-unwell-by-benefits-system.

Noble, K. (2011), *All of Me: How I learned to live with the many personalities sharing my body*, London: Hachette.

Norman, S.B. and Maguen, S. (2020) *Moral Injury. PTSD*: National Center for PTSD, US Department of Veteran Affairs. Retrieved from www.ptsd.va.gov/professional/treat/cooccurring/moral_injury.asp.

Ogden, P. and Fisher, J. (2015), *Sensorimotor Psychotherapy: Interventions for trauma and attachment*, New York: Norton.

Orbach, S. (2002), 'The False Self and the False Body', in *The Legacy of Winnicott: Essays on infant and child mental health*, Kahr, B. (ed.), London: Karnac Books.

Owen, J. (2016), 'Deepcut: Allegations point to "culture of cruelty" where sexual assaults and rape were widespread at army barracks', 15 January, *The Independent*.

Perry, B. (1994), 'Neurobiological Sequelae of Childhood Trauma: PTSD in children', in Murburg, M. (ed.), *Catecholamine Function in Post Traumatic Stress Disorder: Emerging concepts*, pp. 253–76. Washington, DC: American Psychiatric Press.

Phillips, A. (1995), *Terror and Experts*, p. 34, London: Faber & Faber.

Polchar, J., Sweijs, T., Marten, P. and Galdiga, J. (2014), *LGBT Military Personnel: A strategic vision for inclusion*. The Hague, The Netherlands: The Hague Centre for Strategic Studies.

Private Eye (2015), Deepcut deaths: Blocking tactics, April, no. 1390, 17–30, p. 32.

Pynoos, R and Naker, K. (1988), 'Children's Memory and Proximity to Violence'. *Journal of the American Academy of Child and Adolescent Psychiatry*, 28(2), 236–41.

Pynoos, R. and Naker, K. (1993), 'Issues in the Treatment of Post-Traumatic Stress in Children and Adolescents', in Wilson, J.P. and Raphael, B. (eds), *International Handbook of Traumatic Stress Syndromes*, New York: Plenum.

Read, J. (2010), 'Can Poverty Drive You Mad? "Schizophrenia", socio-economic status and the case for primary prevention', *New Zealand Journal of Psychology*, 39(2), 7–19.

Reinders, A.A.T.S., Willemsen, A.T.M., Vos, H.P.J., den Boer, J.A. and Nijenhuis, E.R.S. (2012), 'Fact or Fictitious? A psychobiological study of authentic and simulated dissociative identity states', *PLoS ONE*, vol. 7, no. 7.

Robertson, J. and Robertson, J. (1952) *A Two Year Old Goes To Hospital*, Robertson Films.

Robertson, J. and Robertson, J. (1971), 'Young Children in Brief Separation: A fresh look', *The Psychoanalytic Study of the Child*, 26(1), 264–315.

Rothschild, B. (2000), *The Body Remembers: The psychophysiology of trauma and trauma treatment*, New York: Norton.

Rothschild, B. (2011), *Trauma Essentials: The go-to guide*, New York: Norton.

Sachs, A. (2017), 'Through the Lens of Attachment Relationship: Stable DID, active DID and other trauma-based mental disorders', *Journal of Trauma and Dissociation*, 18(3): The Abused and the Abuser: Victim-perpetrator dynamics.

Sachs, A. (2018), 'Infanticidal Attachment: The link between dissociative identity disorder and crime', in Galton, G and Sachs, A. (eds), *Forensic*

Aspects of Dissociative Identity Disorder, London: Taylor & Francis.

Sachs, A. and Galton, G. (2018) (eds), *Forensic Aspects of Dissociative Identity Disorder*, London: Taylor & Francis.

Sanderson, C. (2020), *The Bystander Effect: The psychology of courage and inaction*, London: HarperCollins.

Santayana, G. (1905), *The Life of Reason: Reason in common sense*, p. 284.

Schaverien, J. (2015), *Boarding School Syndrome*, London: Routledge.

Schlenger W.E., Kulka, R.A., Fairbank, J.A., Hough, R.L., Jordan, B.K., Marmar, C.R. and Weiss, D.S. (1992), 'The Prevalence of PTSD in the Vietnam Generation: A multimethod multisource assessment of psychiatric disorder', *Journal of Traumatic Stress*, 5, 333–64.

Schore, A. (2003), *Affect Regulation and the Repair of the Self* (Norton Series on Interpersonal Neurobiology), New York: Norton.

Schore, A. (2019), *The Development of the Unconscious Mind* (Norton Series on Interpersonal Neurobiology), New York: Norton.

Shakespeare, W. (1623), First folio: 'Fear no more the Heat o' sun', *Cymbeline*, Act IV, Scene 2.

Shepherd, L.J. (2008), *Gender, Violence and Security*, London: Zed Books.

Sinason, V. (1990), 'Passionate Lethal Attachments', *British Journal of Psychotherapy*, 7(1).

Sinason, V. (1992), *Mental Handicap and the Human Condition: New approaches from the Tavistock*, London: Free Association Books.

Sinason, V. (ed.) (1994), *Treating Survivors of Satanist Abuse*, London: Routledge.

Sinason, V. (ed.) (2002), *Attachment, Trauma and Multiplicity*, London: Routledge.

Sinason, V. (2003a) Learning Disability as Trauma and the Impact of Trauma on Learning Disability, PhD, 7.27. St George's Hospital Medical school, University of London.

Sinason, V. (2003b) (ibid) 1.3.2, pp. 1–4.

Sinason, V. (ed.) (2011), *Attachment, Trauma and Multiplicity*, 2nd edn, London: Routledge.

Sinason, V. (ed.) (2012), 'Carole', in *Trauma, Dissociation and Multiplicity. Working on identity and selves*, p. 7, London: Routledge.

Sinason, V. (2014), 'Fairbairn: Abuse, trauma and multiplicity', in Clarke, G.S. and Scharff, D.E. (eds), *Fairbairn and the Object Relations Tradition*, pp.197–208, London: Karnac Books.

Sinason, V. (2017), 'Dying for Love: An attachment problem with some per-
    petrator introjects', *Journal of Trauma and Dissociation*, 18(3), 340–55.

Sinason, V. and Aduale, A. (2008), 'Definition of ritual abuse', talk given
    on Safeguarding London's Children.

Sinason, V. and Conway, A. (2020), *Trauma and Memory: The science and
    the silenced*, London: Routledge.

Sivers, S., Schooler, J. and Freyd, J. (2002) 'Recovered Memories', in
    Ramachandran, V.S. (ed.) *Encyclopedia of the Human Brain*, vol. 4,
    pp. 169–84, Cambridge, MA.: Academic Press/Elsevier.

Sjoberg, L. and Gentry, C.E. (2008), 'Reduced to Bad Sex: Narratives of
    violent women from the Bible to the War on Terror', in *International
    Relations*, 22,(1), 5–23.

Spitz, R. (1945), 'Hospitalism: An inquiry into the genesis of psychiatric con-
    ditions in early childhood', *Psychoanalytic Study of the Child*, 1(1), 53–74.

Spring, C. (2012), 'What Are the Usual Responses to Trauma?', www.
    information.pods-online.org.uk.

Stachowitsch, S. (2012a), *Gender Ideologies and Military Labor Markets in
    the US*, London and New York: Routledge.

Stachowitsch, S. (2012b), 'Professional Soldier, Weak Victim, Patriotic
    Heroine', in *International Feminist Journal of Politics*. Epub ahead of
    print edition 24 July. DOI: 10.1080/14616742.2012.699785.

Stachowitsch, S. (2012c), 'Military Gender Integration and Foreign Policy
    in the United States: A Feminist international relations perspective', in
    Security Dialogue, 43(4), 305–21.

Stachowitsch, S. (2013), 'Feminism and the Current Debates on Women
    in Combat', E-International Relations website, 19 February.

Stark, E.A. and Kringelbach, M.L. (2015), 'Post-traumatic Stress Influ-
    ences the Brain even in the Absence of Symptoms: A systematic,
    quantitative meta-analysis of neuroimaging studies', *Neuroscience and
    Biobehavioral Reviews*, vol. 56, Sept., 207–21.

Steinberg, M. (1994a), *Structured Clinical Interview for DSM-IV Dissocia-
    tive Disorders (SCID-D)*, Washington, DC: American Psychiatric Press.

Steinberg, M. (1994b), *Interviewer's Guide to the Structured Clinical Inter-
    view for DSM-IV Dissociative Disorders (SCID-D)*, Washington, DC:
    American Psychiatric Press.

Steinberg, M. (1995), *Handbook for the Assessment of Dissociation: A clini-
    cal guide*, Washington, DC: American Psychiatric Press.

References

Steinberg, M. and Schnall, M. (2000), *The Stranger in the Mirror: Dissociation – The hidden epidemic*, New York: HarperCollins.

Stephen, L. (ed.) (1886), *Oxford Dictionary of National Biography*, vol. 6, p. 159, London: Macmillan.

Szasz, T. (1961), *The Myth of Mental Illness: Foundations of a theory of personal conduct*, New York: Harper & Row.

Szasz, T. (1970), *The Manufacture of Madness: A comparative study of the inquisition and the mental health movement*, New York: Harper & Row.

United Nations (2018), 'Children Faced with Unspeakable Violence in Conflict as Number of Grave Violations Increased in 2017', *Annual Report of the Secretary-General on Children and Armed Conflict (CAAC)*, 27 June.

Van der Hart, O., Nijenuis, E.R.S. and Steele, K. (2006), *The Haunted Self: Structural dissociation and the treatment of chronic traumatisation*, New York: Norton.

Van der Kolk, B.A. (2015), *The Body Keeps the Score: Brain, mind and body in the transformation of trauma*, New York: Viking.

Van der Kolk, B.A. and Greenberg, M. (1987), 'The Psychobiology of the Trauma Response: Hyperarousal, constriction, and addiction to traumatic response', in Van der Kolk, B.A. (ed.), *Psychological Trauma*, Washington DC: American Psychiatric Press.

Van IJzendoorn, M.H. (1995), 'Adult Attachment Representations, Parental Responsiveness, and Infant Attachment: A meta-analysis on the predictive validity of the adult attachment interview', *Psychological Bulletin*, 117(3), 387–403.

Van Velsen, C. (1997), 'Psychoanalytic Models of PTSD', in Black, D. *et al.* (eds), *Psychological Trauma: A Developmental Approach*, London: The Royal College of Psychiatrists.

Waters, E., Merrick, S., Albersheim, L., Treboux, D. and Crowell, J. (1995), *From the Strange Situation to the Adult Attachment Interview: A 20-year longitudinal study of attachment security in infancy and early adulthood*. Paper presented at the Society for Research in child development, Indianapolis, May.

Wilde, O. (1895), *The Importance of being Ernest*, Act II, Miss Prism.

Winnicott, D.W. (1960), 'Ego Distortions in Terms of True and False Self' in *The Maturational Processes and the Facilitating Environment*, London: Karnac Books.

RESOURCES

Clinic for Dissociative Studies
Help & enquiries:
T: 020 7794 1655
E: info@clinicds.com

European Society for the Study of Trauma and Dissociation (ESTD)
www.estd.org

First Person Plural (FPP)
www.firstpersonplural.org.uk

International Society for the Study of Trauma and Dissociation (ISSTD)
Isstdworld.isst-d.org

National Association for People Abused in Childhood (NAPAC)
napac.org.uk

Positive Outcome for DID (PODS)
https://information.pods-online.org.uk

The Pottergate Centre
176 Wellesley Avenue South,
Norwich NR1 4AD
T: 01603 660029
E: Pottergate Centre

Survivors Trust
www.thesurvivorstrust.org

Tavistock Clinic Trauma Unit
T: 020 7435 7111

INDEX

Index

The Brain has a Mind of its Own

Attachment, Neurobiology, and the New Science of Psychotherapy

Jeremy Holmes

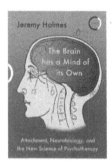

Describing the neuroscientific basis for effective psychotherapy, Professor Holmes draws on the Free Energy Principle, which holds that, through 'active inference' -- agency and model revision -- the brain minimises discrepancies between incoming experience and its pre-existing picture of the world. Difficulties with these processes underlie clients' need for psychotherapeutic help. Using his relational 'borrowed brain' model, the author clearly shows us how the 'talking cure' reinstates active inference and thus how therapy helps bring about change.

ISBN 978-1-913494-02-5 (pbk)   ISBN 978-1-913494-03-2 (e-book)   208 Pages   £12.99

Body Psychotherapy for the 21st Century

Nick Totton

Body psychotherapy currently attracts more interest than ever before, bringing awareness of embodiment into what has been a verbally oriented profession. The approach has developed to engage with other fields including neuroscience, phenomenology, and cognitive studies, as well as the relational turn in psychotherapy. Using a historical survey to chart this transformation, the author shows how four distinct versions of embodied practice have interacted to generate the current field.

ISBN 978-1-913494-04-9 (pbk)   ISBN 978-1-913494-05-6 (e-book)   168 Pages   £12.99

www.confer.uk.com